How To Get Over a Breakup

The Step-by-Step Guide to Getting Over A Broken Heart & Starting Again.

Polly Moretti & David Baxter

2

© Copyright 2020 - All rights reserved.

It is not legal to reproduce, duplicate, or transmit any part of this document in either electronic means or in printed format. Recording of this publication is strictly prohibited and any storage of this document is not allowed unless with written permission from the publisher except for the use of brief quotations in a book review.

Table of Contents

How To Get Over a Breakup..1

The Step-by-Step Guide to Getting Over A Broken Heart & Starting Again...1

Introduction..7

Chapter One: It's Really Over..13

Chapter Two: The Breakup Detox.....................................25

Chapter Three: Protecting Yourself With Social Media .47

Chapter Four: Don't Rush Into The Dating Game Too Soon..60

Chapter Five: Rebuild your Self-Esteem..........................79

Chapter Six: The Dos and Don'ts After a Breakup 103

Chapter Seven: Rethink your Definition of Closure.......121

Chapter Eight: Finally, Forgive and Move on 130

Conclusion 138

Sources 139

6

Introduction

Breakups are terrible. They can shake you to the core, causing you to question your confidence and faith in love. Even in the most amicable and mutual situations, a breakup is an ending. In a culture that upholds *"forever"* as the ultimate relationship goal, a breakup could make you feel like you failed.

Your heart might be broken, but you don't have to break with it. This book urges you to rethink how you deal with a breakup, offering wise, warm, and witty advice to get over the split. The healing process begins with a choice, a determination to move on, even when your mind is fighting it. This book offers actionable insights to take control of your life and put yourself on the right path to healing.

The real pain of a breakup

The pain induced by a breakup doesn't correlate with the overall quality of the relationship. You're probably asking, *"why do I feel so hurt, the relationship wasn't that great?"* The angst associated with relationship issues is compounded by different factors that correlate to the attachment.

Everyone has a unique style of relating to other people. This attachment style stems from one's early experiences with their parents. If your parents were consistently responsive to your early needs, the chances are that you still believe you are worthy of love. You have a somewhat secure sense of self and can access your deeper emotions because you feel secure.

For instance, your experiences of empathy allow you to be empathetic. You can understand and trust your partner's feelings and perspectives. Caring deeply for your partner means you have developed a strong attachment with that person.

On the other hand, if one's early emotional and physical needs were not responded to consistently, the chances are that they will find it hard to trust other people. They resurrect harsh defense mechanisms to protect the fragile self. In the worst case scenario, such people get preoccupied with their needs at the expense of their loved ones.

Additionally, they exercise a higher level of dominance and control to feel secure and comfortable in a relationship. This style of attachment is known as anxious or avoidant. Extreme egocentrism forces such people to attach superficially in addition to putting their needs first.

Emotional pain

No matter the attachment style, a breakup is a severing of that bond. It is a terrible nightmare after having an exciting dream. When two people fall in love, they share unique elements of who they are. They become aware of what's important to one another and validate those elements. This is how a bond between two partners begins to solidify.

Feeling understood, known, and appreciated creates a form of attachment. The moment that bond is severed, you lose these *"good feelings,"* which causes you to feel more vulnerable in your sense of self. As a result, you may feel confused, isolated, or sad. It's not just the absence of your partner that makes you feel hurt. The deficit in your identity that a severed bond creates could hurt you too. All these issues evoke a high level of emotional pain.

Another type of angst associated with a breakup occurs when the attachment is heavy for one person and superficial for the other. In essence, the person with anxious or avoidant attachment pretends to care, know, and validate their partner to woo and reel them in. It's more about manipulation to gain more control instead of genuine care.

In such a situation, the party that attaches superficially can sever the relations without a second thought. They don't care what happens next or to the other person. Unfortunately, the person with a heavy attachment feels the impact of severed bonds profoundly. The hurt is compounded when this person realizes that their ex-partner doesn't feel the loss at all and can move on easily. Feelings of abandonment in this situation elicit intense emotional anguish.

Physical pain

A breakup is also referred to as *"heartbreak"* and for a good reason. It causes physical pain. Many people think of a breakup as purely emotional, but forget its physical dimension. Some people feel chest pain, stomachaches, or other pain in their bodies.

Social scientists firmly believe that this phenomenon has been around for many years[1]. Just like grief, your psychological response to social rejection is triggered by your deepest survival instincts. People are like a herd of animals who rely on each other to survive. Our brains have developed a form of a physical alarm system to warn us whenever we get too far from people we care about. This keeps us from drifting away, even when we disagree.

---

[1] (n.d.). Why Does Social Exclusion Hurt? - Semantic Scholar. Retrieved July 22, 2020, from https://pdfs.semanticscholar.org/0e71/1c40ec38b531215de3ed80a26fe08eb7d0f6.pdf

Social rejection hijacks that part of your brain. It tells you, *"hey, this is a serious situation, just like physical pain, there are consequences."*

Today, you don't need tribe members to help you fight off tigers. However, you need other people to get through some issues in your life. Recent studies at the University of Arizona and UCLA reveal that humans are better off, mentally and physically, when we are in strong social relationships. Loneliness triggers stress cardiomyopathy, commonly known as heartbreak syndrome. In extreme cases, emotional stressors can cause a healthy person to develop issues like a heart attack.

If you are experiencing social rejection like a breakup, physical pain is a sign to step back and be mindful of your health. Just think about it, if your muscles become sore after pushing your body too far during a workout, what would you do?

Heartache is a functional response saying to you, *"Look, something has happened."* Though breakups hurt, they also provide an opportunity to learn, if only you are willing to listen. Take a moment to stop, understand what happened, and establish new connections with people who make you feel better. Thinking too much about the damaged relationship worsens the physical pain, and that's something you definitely don't want.

Dented self-esteem

Even for situations where severed relationships are forthcoming, for example, if one of the partners cheated, or there were simply just endless arguments, the impact on the other party who quits the relationship goes through an emotional roller coaster ride. No matter the cause of the split, one of the partners will feel unloved or even worthless. This is when reality and expectations collide.

When you fall in love with someone, there are some expectations from both sides. When these expectations are not met, mistrust and disputes arise.

Ending a relationship that you adored can leave you feeling empty. You will want to figure out why things didn't go as planned. The desire to gather information and avoid future mistakes is unavoidable. However, the rationale behind the disintegrating relationship is seldom black and white. It can be very challenging for your brain to process.

Generally, people tend to find comfort in logic and their ability to pinpoint the primary cause of the breakup. Unfortunately, romantic relationships are complex equations with many variables. It's always challenging to define what, when, and how everything went awry. Unless you have concrete information that is not articulated, you will start blaming yourself and feel that the shattered relationship is a reflection of you.

In your quest to backtrack and figure out what didn't work, you will begin to see how much you failed. This can negatively affect your self-esteem.

Do you have to feel this forever?

The pain and amount of loss associated with a breakup make sense if you think about it in relation to attachment towards the other person. A severed relationship may affect your sense of self, make you feel abandoned, and in some cases, cause a loss of hope for a better future.

Sometimes, love hurts. But it doesn't have to hurt forever. Hang in there; there are many ways to get over a breakup and live a better life. In the long run, personal growth is associated with breakups such as increased independence, a more active social life, a healthier lifestyle, and a better relationship with other people. So, maybe nature and your loved ones were right – your breakup could be the beginning of a brighter future.

Summary

Breakup? Check.

Heartache? Check.

But you're no longer confused.

You now know what breakups are, the pain they cause, and why they hurt so much. No matter how much you feel hurt, don't let anger, resentment, and negative feelings stop you from letting go and starting over.

It's not going to be easy. But this book is a simple blueprint to help you get over a severed attachment. It will help you understand your emotions and find a way to a better life after break up.

Let's get started!

Chapter One: It's *Really* Over

Love is the most profound emotion known to humans. There are many types of love, but most people, no matter their age, seek it in romantic relationships with the right partner. These relationships comprise meaningful aspects of life and offer a deep source of fulfillment. The need for human-to-human connection is somewhat innate, but the ability to form loving and healthy relationships is learned.

The ability to form stable relationships begins in infancy. Think about a child's earliest relationship with a parent or a caregiver. That caregiver meets the child's needs for protection, food, care, warmth, and social contact. These relationships are not destiny. Instead, they are theorized to form deeply ingrained patterns of connecting or relating to others.

Failed relationships happen for different reasons. The failure of your relationship isn't the same as the crumbling of your best friend's marriage. A failed relationship isn't an indication of your inability to love or be loved. Love isn't always black and white, it is a million shades of grey. What works for your friend may not work for you.

Your body's reaction to a breakup

Getting over a breakup is a challenging process. In the first few (sometimes brutal) weeks, you have every right to feel sad and even inconsolable. Take the time to grieve, accept that you cannot control everything, trust that you will not feel this forever, make the right choices to protect your heart, and finally, accept that it's over. This is the foundation of deep healing.

Grieving after a breakup and what to expect

You may have fought hard to hold on to the relationship, even to the point of being all-consumed by it. It's hard to believe that something you wanted so much slipped from your fingers. Even if the relationship wasn't always a smooth ride, the idea of living without your significant other may feel unbearable.

Still, it's beyond any reasonable doubt that the two of you are not going to make it, and you're finally beginning to understand that it's really over. Perhaps your thoughts are shifting from *"please don't leave"* to *"this might be okay."*

It is an unfortunate truth that a breakup, in any form, can put you in an emotional tailspin. Whether a minor rejection or a full-blown, life-changing issue like divorce, a breakup can put you through an emotional roller coaster.

The moment you leave each other's space, get off the phone with your ex, or the texting stops, things will change. The chances are that you will be hit relentlessly by withdrawals and the reality of loss. A million questions and possibilities will race through your mind. *"What went wrong?" "Can we fix it?"* And… *"Why are you such an idiot?"* These are all valid questions that skate through your mind and probably tug at your heartstrings. It is a brutal process that can take a long time… unless you know how to get over it.

You may have suspected that the breakup was coming for weeks or even months. No matter how the lead-up looked, you're now dealing with the aftermath of the split. It is okay to feel fear, loss, or despair about your new life without your significant other. However, knowing what to expect during the grieving process can ease the pain and frustration you are facing. Below, we'll discuss some of the things you should expect. Keep in mind, these might occur all at once or at varying times. It is hard to predict a broken heart.

Relentless urge to get answers: You really want to know what went wrong. The drive to know can be consuming and often comes at the expense of rational behavior and thoughts. The urge to know the main cause of the breakup may be beyond your ability to comprehend. You probably fixate on your ex's words that you see contradicting the split and hold on to them. Yet, you still may find that you have moments of clarity.

The chances are that you will swing back and forth between the moment-by-moment realization of your loss, foggy disbelief, and flashes of painful truth that the union is over. The disorganization, pain, and confusion might dominate your thoughts and become all that you talk about. In the worst-case scenario, the desperation to make sense of everything might compel you to debate with friends, colleagues, family, and even strangers about why the breakup shouldn't have happened.

Sure, you want answers, but that doesn't mean you should obsess over it. Don't take the issue too far.

Bargaining: Sometimes, it's hard to let go. You promise yourself you will become a more attentive and caring partner. The mere thought of breakup is so intolerable that you just want to make your pain go away by just winning your ex back, at all costs.

At this point, you're not logical. It's like you're standing on the edge of an abyss and trying to avoid falling into the unknown. It feels like you are clinging to any shred of hope to avoid losing what you've come to rely on, for better for worse.

The moment you start trying to fix all the problems between you and your ex, you will be placing the burden of maintaining, repairing, and sustaining the union onto yourself. You will become responsible for making the relationship work this time. This is wrong. You cannot take responsibility for everything, and somewhere inside, you already know this.

Bargaining will briefly distract you from the pain of loss. But the reality is inevitable and will come crashing down on you. Besides, bargaining means you're taking responsibility for the issues that led to the crumbling of your relationship. This might result in the illusion that you have everything under control, perpetuating the idea that you can still save the relationship. This will intensify the heartache once you realize that your partner isn't coming back.

Denial: *"This isn't happening!"* *"It can't be true!"* Does this sound familiar? Does the thought of a life without your ex send a cold shiver down your spine? Perhaps the relationship was your life, your world. Now that you're losing it, you cannot accept that it's over. Attempts to funnel your last hope into saving a severed relationship could impact your well-being. Indeed, you will derail the grieving process if you replace acceptance with unrealistically inflated hope that you can still salvage the relationship.

Denying a breakup can help you feel better in the short term. However, you are eventually going to have to face the hard facts and come to terms with the split in the future. It is in your best interest to get out of the self-denial rut and get ready to face the world.

The urge to reach out to your ex in the weeks or months following a split is compelling and can make it more challenging for you to move on. Don't give in. Instead, give yourself a time limit, which you'll commit to not reaching your ex in any way. Whether it is two weeks or two months, setting a period when you will not try to reach out to your ex in any way can be helpful in getting out of the denial pit.

Anger: During a breakup, anger takes many forms. At first, it can be more like self-blame. You will get angry at yourself for what you perceive as messing up the relationship. You will probably say, *"I deserved it!"* This kind of anger could also be self-disgust. You will start thinking that you are fat, old, stupid, useless, or worse. Self-blame and self-disgust are immobilizing and unproductive forms of anger. Trust me, it's a long way out of the abyss you are throwing yourself into.

Getting angry at your ex-partner for the demise of your relationship means you are trying to make sense of what happened. Typically, you are trying to determine who is to blame or who was most at fault. No matter whose fault it was, blaming your ex, or yourself for that matter, will not change the outcome.

Healing and progress come when you start recognizing that you are angry about the ending of your relationship. Sure, it's unjust and unfair, but it's reality. Being responsible for your anger makes it easy to reunify the *"pieces of you"* that shattered during the events leading to the split. This approach can give you a way forward.

The process of grieving after a breakup takes different forms. This is because the emotional responses to severed relationships vary greatly from person to person. Sometimes, it can be hard to tell if whatever you are feeling is just a natural response to the loss of something you adored or if your anger is getting out of control.

Sadness and grief are normal reactions after stressful life events like a breakup or a divorce. Other healthy responses include crying, regret, and frustration. However, you should be careful not to let these emotions dictate your life and influence your decision making moving forward.

The grieving period is your chance to make the right adjustments. So, give yourself some time to reflect on what matters to you and focus on healing.

You will not feel this way forever

You are probably not ready to hear this yet. Perhaps everything seems to be heading south. But you will get through it. Even if your world seems to be caving in, there is always nature's wake-up call. Don't snooze it, please.

A severed relationship can be the turning point for a bright future that could be better than anything you had in the past. The union (and maybe your life) was not all you wanted to be. Perhaps you were happy with it, but your ex-partner wasn't. No matter the root cause for the split, the relationship was not built on a foundation solid enough to sustain it.

There is nothing wrong with that. The key to healing after a breakup is taking control and owning your own life. Believe it or not, there is a psychological process for this. It's known as acceptance. Living in anger, regret, anxiety, or fear will hinder you from moving forward.

The power of acceptance

"Of course, there is no formula for success except, perhaps, an unconditional acceptance of life and what it brings"
Arthur Rubinstein

We observe other people's lives and think we may never experience some of the nasty issues they face. We may say, *"that will never happen to me."* After all, positive affirmations are a powerful way to release yourself from fear, anxiety, and negativity.

Part of the beauty of nature is that it's unpredictable. Nothing is permanent, and of course, many things can happen that will transform who you are. We have all experienced changes in our lives, both expected and unexpected, good and bad. Circumstances, relationships, and feelings change. No one is ever the same at each moment.

Life can bring many changes. Academic excellence, a bright career, true love, and family unions are some of the good things we want. At the same time, life can deliver a devastating blow to your life. For example, breakups or the death of a loved one are hard to embrace. For weeks or months, we suffer and wish those things never happened.

It's banal to say that the most interesting thing about change is its irony. It is the one constant in human life, the only thing that never changes. Yet, most of us don't have a healthy relationship with change. We neither want it nor like it. We rarely seek it, and more often than not, we resist it. There's no escaping this fundamental fact of human existence: change happens.

The first and most important step in getting over a breakup is to cultivate the ability to accept what has happened in your life and embrace it. Yes, acceptance is a choice – a hard one, but a good choice nonetheless.

In the wake of heartbreak, there are two ways out of the problem. First, accept what happened, see the positive aspects of the split, and choose a peaceful state of mind. Alternatively, you can fight against it, live a miserable life, and struggle against the universe for months or even years.

Acceptance is the key to convert momentary happiness to long-term happiness. It prepares you to live in a constantly changing world, where no one is absolutely sure of what's coming tomorrow. Practicing acceptance is protecting your emotional and mental health.

Learn to accept

The concept of acceptance isn't about weakness. It's not a synonym for mediocrity or conformity. We all need to master the art of identifying when it's safe to persist and when to accept. If you choose to find out what caused the breakup, be careful not to keep on blaming yourself. Otherwise, it will do more harm than good.

Choose not to judge yourself and what happened. Instead, believe that everything happened for a reason, and better things are coming your way. This is the beginning of acceptance.

Never let fear rule

Heartbreak and the changes associated with it are scary. The black cloud of uncertainty that shadow life during and after a breakup is scary. Humans are hardwired to crave comfort and only think of a *"bad change"* when something isn't working.

How many times have you said or heard someone say, *"If it's not broken, don't fix it?"* There's a common misconception that change must happen only when something (like your relationship) is broken and should be fixed. Fixing, in this context, is not always a black and white solution. Sometimes, letting go could be the best solution.

If you want to make a change that could make you feel better about yourself, don't be scared of doing something. If you are in a toxic relationship or going through a breakup, the chances are that you are desperate for a change. Don't let the fear of loss or the unknown dictate your life.

The worst part about fear is that the forces holding you back are nearly always something you have developed from insecurity or simply your mindset. Indeed, they are things conjured in your mind, and you even don't know their origin. The insecurity in your mind just nibbles at you, and when the moment comes for it to reveal its ugly face, you find yourself regretting every choice you've ever made. For example, you just parted ways with someone you truly loved. The thought of a new life without that person can be terrifying, and it hurts. You have to overcome that fear. Here's how.

Identify your fear

First, take a deep breath and clear your mind. Figure out what you are afraid of. For instance, are you afraid of being alone, of financial issues, of receiving blame from relatives, or being unable to attract the right partner in the future? As you reflect on your fears, you will find some clues about how you can start overcoming them. For example, if you are afraid of being alone, you can start spending some time with your friends.

Self-compassion

Once you figure out what you are afraid of, don't respond to that fear with harsh self-criticism. Don't blame yourself for not being attractive enough or being the cause of the breakup. Avoid name-calling yourself like, *"I'm such a loser."* Instead, practice self-compassion.

Think about helping a kid who is afraid of his first day of school. You would say something like, *"it will be okay"* or *"you will make many friends, and your teachers will help you."* That kid will feel supported and encouraged. This approach can help you practice self-compassion after a breakup.

Face your fear

You are afraid, and it's okay to feel scared, but recognize that's just an emotion. Don't let it dictate everything you do. Practice positive thinking, self-support, and trust that you will get through this hard time. Make the decision to stay strong and tell yourself, *"I can do this."*

At the same time, avoid beating your fear into submission. Suppressing your fear might work for a little while, but you will end up feeling like you failed in the long run. Choose a caring approach when dealing with your fears. Self-compassion will give you the courage you need to confront your fear successfully.

Embrace the unknown

Certainty is an illusion.

Let's be honest, is there ever a moment you were absolutely sure how things would unfold? Even with the most effective preparation, you cannot be sure or control everything in life. Relationships transform as partners grow and change their perspectives on life.

There are no guarantees, even for people who feel that they have everything figured out. Breakups come with a lot of uncertainty, and you don't know what the future will hold. This shouldn't make you anxious. You are actually dealing with life, and it's best to create it moment by moment. Live day by day and stop worrying about who you will fall in love with in the future.

You may find it challenging to forego the attachment or bond you had developed with your ex. The odds are that your partner was an integral part of your desired life – he or she made you feel safe, loved, and comfortable. Clinging to these thoughts won't make the healing process easy. Instead, think of the relationship from a different perspective. As you detach from the relationship, you will start opening yourself to new opportunities.

Another way of embracing the unknown is to reconnect with your life's constants. You may not be sure of what the future holds, but there are things that will not change in the future. These include your mental capacity, friends, health, and family. Nothing matters without these elements. Focus on these gifts because they beautify your life. Instead of worrying about the uncertain future, focus on improving your health, and reconnect with friends and family.

Stay positive and optimistic

As of the time you and your ex decided to enter into an intimate relationship, you were both committed to each other, with no intention of parting ways. A few weeks, months, or maybe even years down the line, things didn't work out as expected. No matter what happened, there is more to life than questioning your ability to love or be loved. Instead, focus on thinking positively and being optimistic. Here are a few tips.

Mourn – allow yourself to feel the pain

You have been hurt, and you need to allow yourself to feel that. Don't suppress your feelings and pretend that everything is okay. It is normal to feel hurt because you spent a lot of time, effort, and emotion on your ex. What matters is your approach to cope up with that pain. Let it be your strength to usher in the stronger you, the best version of yourself.

Do something new

Travel or do something adventurous, like surfing or hiking. If you are not into sports, go to a painting or pottery class. Do something that you've never done before. It is an amazing feeling to learn and do something new. At first, it might feel scary, but you'll never know unless you try it. Just don't get a breakup haircut. I will tell you why later.

Just accept it, it's over

The relationship is gone. The change forced itself upon your life, and you cannot control it. It's a shock, and it's okay to feel blindsided. As much as you want to think things can still work, it's best to accept that you and ex aren't getting back to each other.

Chapter Two: The Breakup Detox

"Love is like a drug, and we don't care about the long-term side effects; we just care about how high we can get"
Unknown

Accumulating scientific evidence suggests that romantic love can be addictive. The exact nature of the link between love and addiction is often described in inconsistent terms in modern literature. This chapter will help you understand the narrow view and broad perspective of love addiction. Also, the chapter will offer you a comprehensive guide to overcoming this addiction – breakup detox.

Love addiction

"By nature, we are all addicted to love….meaning we want it, seek it, and have a hard time not thinking about it. We need an attachment to survive, and we instinctively seek connection, especially romantic connection. But there is nothing dysfunctional about wanting love."
Smith

Throughout history, love has been perceived as an excruciating passion. Ovid once proclaimed, *"I can't live with or without you."* This locution was made famous to modern ears by U2, an Irish band. Contemporary films express similar sentiments. For example, Jake Gyllenhaal in *Brokeback Mountain* says, *"I wish I knew how to quit you."*

Everyday speech is rife with unique expressions such as *"I'm addicted to you"* or *"I need you."* These commonly used expressions capture the fact that when you fall in love, you get an overwhelmingly strong attraction to your partner. That feeling is persistent and hard to ignore.

Love is thrilling and can be perilous sometimes. When your feelings are reciprocated, you might feel euphoric. Love's pull can also be so strong that you might follow it to the point of personal ruin and hardships. Other times, lovers can be unreliable, distracted, unfaithful, and unreasonable. When a relationship snaps, pain, loss, and grief are inevitable. The chances are that you will experience withdrawal and become depressed.

There are cycles of alternating ecstasy and desperate longing, despair, and damaging thoughts or behavior that follow a lover's loss. It is a phenomenon that bears a resemblance to an analogous phenomenon linked to *"conventional"* addictions like those for drugs and gambling.

Though the language of addiction is often used to describe love, there's at least one distinguishing feature that's not associated with substance-based addictions described in medical and psychological literature. Everyone desires to fall in love. By contrast, nobody aspires to become addicted to slot machines, heroin, and alcohol. It seems absurd to argue that there could be a similarity between drug addicts and lovers.

So could the concept of love addiction be hyperbole and somewhat poetic?

Perhaps not. There are numerous superficial similarities between love-based interpersonal attachments and addictive substance use. Some of these similarities include ecstasy, craving, exhilaration, obsessive thinking patterns, and irregular psychological responses. This is the primary reason some scientific theorists have started to argue that both phenomena might rely upon similar chemical, psychological, and neuroanatomical substrates.

This concept isn't hard to understand. Just think about it; you often feel some sort of excitement, attraction, and deep connection whenever interacting with someone you love. That makes love and relationships a powerful force that affects your brain in different ways. You may know when the bond between you and your partner is flourishing, and how terrible it might be during and after a breakup.

Love withdrawal hurts

Love is like a drug. It can make you happy or drive you mad. Despite how much you loved your partner, it's inevitable that you have to move on. That's a logical decision, and probably one of the hardest choices you have had to make. Does that make it easier to stop loving them? Your ex's hugs gave you comfort, their smiles lit you up, and that gentle touch made you quiver. You might even say you were addicted to his or her love.

Often, addictions rule over emotions, and it's difficult to rationalize them. This is the main reason you are reaching out to your ex. When they respond, you promise each other that you won't talk anymore. You decide to give each other space, but a few days later, you still want to *"talk things out."*

You are just going in circles! Nothing has changed. You are both blinded by love. Justifying your actions and hoping that everything will fix itself magically won't work. It's time you kick the toxic habit and overcome your addiction to your partner.

The term toxic means *"being poisonous, especially when being able to cause serious debilitation."* It is often used to describe chemicals, however, it can also be used to describe relationships and people. Toxicity comes in many forms – physical abuse, gossip, name-calling, and the internal turmoil associated with heartbreak or unhealthy relationships.

There's still something that binds you to that person who hurt you. It is the thing that you still miss from the partner that caused you so much pain. There is also the curiosity evoked by your ex even after they left you. This inexplicable sadness keeping you up at night and filling your days is neither madness nor a sign that the breakup was the wrong choice. It's all a product of sexual energy that continues to connect you emotionally to your ex, even if you don't love them anymore.

It's time you start moving forward, knock on other doors, and crack some windows open to let in the sunshine. You need a post-breakup detox to a better, healthier, and more sane YOU. Here are the important steps you must follow.

Step 1: Disengage and delete everything

Now that the relationship has run its course, you desperately need someone to talk to. A person who understands you knows you and a person you can count on to make you feel better. Believe it or not, the first person to click in your mind may be your former partner. This is the no-win situation that inspires people to put their fists through the nearest convenient wall.

Perhaps you don't need your ex to comfort you. You're just doing fine without them. A few days or weeks later, you might be tempted to contact him or her. Besides, the act of calling your ex could tell them that you have become a better person to spend some time with. You just lack the right words to express yourself.

Do you see that trap?

That one person in your world you want to communicate with is the one individual you must cut off all forms of contact with. If you keep communicating with your ex, you will never get the chance to cut emotional ties to them.

One of the most common problems for people who struggle with heartbreak is that they can't stop communicating with their ex-partners. Even after it's clear that the relationship is over, people still find it hard to stop all communication and can't avoid those *"last meetings."* If you're ever going to heal emotionally and fully get over the breakup, disengagement is non negotiable.

Gone are the days when people used to travel on horseback or send letters and wait for a response. Advancements in technology have brought about positive and unprecedented changes in our lives. Today, communication is instant. This is a double-edged sword for people struggling with a breakup. Your ex is just a phone call or text message away. Even if you don't call them, it's easy to run across their social media profiles and posts. And trust me, you will be tempted to check their posts.

This is a hurdle that requires you to steel your resolve. Take a deep breath, calm yourself, and try to get yourself in the right frame of mind to make a bold choice. When you are ready, commit yourself to not getting in touch with your ex for a specific period of time. This communication blackout can last for a month or more, depending on what you deem necessary.

The moment you decide to stop communication with your ex, the chances are that you will want to let them know, particularly if you talk via social media platforms. Write a brief message to your ex. Inform him or her that you need some time away.

Remember, timing is key. Think of the best way and time to communicate your decision to disengage. A relationship isn't a piece of paper on which you can write anything or erase at your convenience. Perhaps your ex isn't on the same page or ready to accept this.

Stopping any kind of reception or just saying goodbye will bring a lot of pain to them. So, don't be too selfish and don't simply go MIA. Instead, let your ex know that disengagement is the best option for each of you, and it's in your mutual interest to say goodbye.

Disengagement takes time. It is a tough process and requires you to be fully committed. Here are some of the top disengagement tips to detach from your ex physically and emotionally.

The no-contact rule: The no contact rule is about shutting down contact or communication with your ex for a specific period. During this period, you will get the space you need to heal. There are many types of no-contact rules, and your choice will depend on different factors. These factors include your main objective, who you are applying it to, and your current situation with that person.

If you choose to apply a no-contact rule to your ex-partner, you must stop communicating with them. Stop contacting them, texting them, or hitting them up on WhatsApp, Facebook, or Snapchat. The same applies if you decide to disengage from a toxic relative. Here are different types of no-contact rules that you should know.

Definite no contact rule AKA "radio silence": This disengagement strategy is intended to help you get a unique perspective after a hurtful breakup. Just think of your ex as an addictive drug, and the only thing you want is to stop that addiction. To achieve this, you must go cold turkey. And that's what "complete radio silence" is all about. Here are a few tips for you:

- No phone calls

- Avoid bumping into your ex accidentally

- No text messages

- Don't go over to his or her house

- Don't contact your ex through his or her friends

- Don't engage them via status messages on Instagram, Facebook, or other social media platforms.

- Don't contact them via Facebook messages or other IM platforms.

The point is to go cold turkey. It's time to learn how to live without your ex. Don't let even a small dose of that person into your life. This is because any form of contact with your ex will remind you of the good times you had, the pain of the severed relationship, and you don't want to reignite those bad feelings again.

At first, you may feel that you are in desperate need of your ex, but don't succumb to those urges. Instead, live your life. Focus on things that make you feel better. Learn to take care of yourself and be your own best friend, because no one else will do all that for you.

The moment you disengage, focus on things that make you happier and more confident. If you used to be happy simply because your partner could cheer you up, you must learn some different ways of being happy without them. The reality is that you will miss your ex at some point, but there is a big difference between needing someone and wanting someone. After a breakup, you neither need nor want your ex.

This change in perspective will not come easily. If you just sit around all day eating ice cream and watching TV, you will never feel better about yourself. Even if every cell in your body desires to stay at home, you must force yourself to get out. Get in touch with your relatives and friends. These are the people who will help you realize that you are still cared about and loved.

It's recommended to participate in activities that can help you relax. Sure, you are going through hard issues, and you're trying your best to cope and get through it. Why don't you spend some quality time rewarding yourself with relaxation? You don't need an overseas holiday to relax. Some of the more affordable ways to relax include massage, meditation, yoga, a spa day, or even a relaxing warm bath.

Don't obsess over your ex during the *"radio silence"* period. You will not be helping yourself if you are watching everything that they are doing. Thinking of your ex once in a while is one thing, but keeping tabs on them is a different story. If you realize you can't keep your eye off ex's movement, take a step back. Find out why you're doing this. Remember, the primary aim of the no-contact rule is to learn to live without your ex, not to continue keeping tabs on them.

Don't indulge in alcohol or other drugs. It is easy to cover up your frustrations and pain that way, but indulging in drugs and other substances never truly heals anything. It will not help you feel better. It's like covering a broken bone with a bandage or replacing one addiction (your love for ex) with another (drugs).

Mild no-contact rule: For some reason, some people cannot avoid their ex-partners. For example, if you still live with your ex, have a child with them, or work with them, the chances are that you will not be able to avoid them entirely. In this situation, the mild no-contact rule works perfectly.

Only speak to your ex about the specific issues that require their attention. Never initiate contact unless there's an important issue. If you're living with your ex, talk to them about the most viable living arrangement and other house-related issues. In every conversation, try to stay objective. If your ex initiates a conversation, reply to them politely. Don't let that conversation continue unnecessarily.

Sometimes, your ex might try to talk to you about something personal. End that conversation immediately, but politely. Just be honest with them and let them know that you need time and space. You can say something like, *"I truly appreciate you letting me know. But I'm still recovering from the previous issues we had, and I would rather not talk about it right now. I hope you understand and appreciate these boundaries. Please let's keep our conversations about work, living arrangements, or our child."*

Whenever there's a conflict, solve it amicably. Take a deep breath and make sure you are calm before you start talking about the issue. Be clear about the specific issue in question, why it needs to be addressed, how it affects you, and what your ex-partner can do to resolve the issue successfully.

If you are still angry about the issue, stay away from that conversation. Be honest with your ex and let them know that you're still upset and unable to discuss it. Suggest that you handle the issue later, when you're ready.

The moment you realize that your ex is becoming unreasonable, don't be afraid of taking serious action. Your ex-partner may try to play games to get a reaction out of you. For instance, they may post things on social media or say something to your friends just to get your attention. Perhaps you work with your ex, and he or she is doing things that make it challenging for you two to work together. You can choose to ignore them. If that won't work, just tell them whatever they are doing is affecting you, and they need to stop.

A brief no-contact rule: The primary purpose of a brief no-contact strategy is to give you time and space to figure out what caused a breakup. It is a chance for you to work on your self-improvement. Generally, it is a risky move, and you need to act carefully. It can work only if;

- You didn't act desperate or needy after the breakup. You simply accepted it and stopped contacting your ex.

- You didn't tell your ex that you never wanted a split. All you did was to hide your true feelings from him or her.

- The main cause of the breakup was something you are currently fixing, or you can fix it within a short period of time.

- Your ex-partner has been trying to contact you for quite some time. They're showing strong signs that they regret the breakup.

The main purpose of a brief no-contact plan is to figure out your ex's stand. Therefore, it's recommended to keep your distance as you figure out what caused the breakup. Don't rush to get back to each other unless you're absolutely sure it will work.

The no-initiate rule: This is a unique version of a no-contact rule. It applies to casual breakups or situations where you didn't act too desperate or needy after a breakup. This rule should be used when you are absolutely sure that interacting with your ex will not negatively affect your emotional health.

Don't initiate contact with your ex-partner. Instead, let them initiate contact. When they do, act politely and respond casually. Don't flirt or send the wrong signals. This is a perfect way to re-establish a connection and attraction with your ex without cutting them off.

Beware, not everyone can do this. In fact, a very small percentage of people who suffered a breakup can interact with their ex-partners without getting hurt. The key here is your emotional health. If you can get close to your ex without regret or anger, you can apply this rule. Here are scenarios where you may use this rule:

- You and your ex-partner were together for a short time, and the breakup wasn't messy.

- You never acted desperate or needy after the relationship ended.

- You and your ex-partner intend to remain friendly. Also, both of you are not invested in the idea of reigniting the love relationship.

- You're already seeing someone else, and your ex is just another option.

The no-initiate rule shouldn't stop you from doing other things you love. Spend quality time with your loved ones, participate in social activities, implement a physical workout program, and undertake activities that will relax your mind. Also, you don't need a hard deadline in case your ex-partner tries to contact you. You can choose to contact your ex whenever you feel that the moment is right.

The indefinite no-contact rule: Well, this disengagement strategy is straightforward. You just end communication with your ex indefinitely. You're not going to contact him or her ever again. This rule can be helpful if you intend to get over a toxic relationship. You must cut off the attachment you had developed towards your ex. At first, you may go through withdrawal-like symptoms, but eventually, you will realize that the relationship wasn't good for you.

Another reason to implement an indefinite no-contact rule is to remove a toxic individual from your life. This could be your ex, a friend, or a relative. Generally, a toxic person could bring you down and doesn't contribute anything positive to your healing process. Getting over a breakup isn't easy, and the last thing you want is someone who does things just to upset you.

Delete everything and get rid of things that remind you of your ex

Breakups in the pre-phone era were somewhat easier than today's. Love letters were torn asunder, scissors were taken to all holiday photographs, keepsakes were boxed away to gather dust, and clothes were boxed and sent to the rightful owner.

The advent of the internet and mobile devices has led to the evolution of relationships and breakups. Today, you have to expunge physical mementos in the wake of a severed relationship and clean up your ex's electronic devices.

Have you ever watched the TV show *Friends*? Do you remember when Phoebe, Monica, and Rachael staged a ritual burning of all photographs and other physical tokens given to them by previous boyfriends? This was the epitome of the post-breakup detox of the pre-phone era. More than 20 years later, the breakup rituals of the digital era are very different.

Delete, delete, delete!

Your computer and phone are all extensions of your space. You have been working so hard to eliminate your ex-partner's influence in your personal space, so delete all text messages, emails, and other forms of digital content revolving around them.

Erase all romantic emojis and photographs from your contact list. For example, you can remove the heart emojis from your ex's name on your phone contact list. You may want to replace it with an unattractive picture of him or her. If your ex's name on your phone is a lovely pet name, replace it with their real name or even something a little bit rude.

You don't have to erase this content forever. You can create a special folder in your cloud storage account, upload all emails, text messages, and media there. Also, you can save his or her number on the same account. Once you have a backup of everything, you need in your cloud storage, erase the content from your phone and computer.

Having photos, text messages, and other media that reminds you of your ex could drag you back and make it more challenging to get over the relationship.

Get rid of things that remind you of your ex

You are trying to move on. But everywhere you turn, there are so many things that remind you of your ex. Even the safest space, like your apartment, reminds you of the person who hurt you. So, what should you do? Sell or throw away everything? How do you make your living space an ex-free zone?

Rearrange

Reorder your space. Shift your bedroom furniture and rearrange your sitting room. The goal is to create a difference between how things were then and how it is today. This is important, particularly if your ex used to spend a lot of time in your apartment. Here are tips for handling things that remind you of your ex-partner.

- Throw out all that stuff that conjures mixed emotions about your ex.

- Put it all in a box and stash it away. Your ex will probably come asking for a thing or two.

- Get rid of the items that you don't use. If you're still comfortable with wearing that stunning necklace your ex gave you, don't throw it away.

The psychology behind erasing pictures of your ex-partner

Erasing pictures of your ex-partner after a breakup says a lot about your emotional and mental state. You can delete the pictures immediately after the breakup or do it beforehand. However, some people never want to erase the experiences they had. They prefer to preserve those experiences and memories.

As mentioned earlier, different people respond to heartache differently. To decide whether you should delete or keep your ex's text messages and photos, think about the benefits and downsides of your choice. How do you feel about erasing the pictures?

Every romantic relationship is unique. If you end a dysfunctional union and photos of your ex revive harsh memories, it's best to delete them. However, if you and your childhood darling broke up because he or she went to a faraway college, you may want to keep the photographs with appreciation, not pain.

What do you think and feel about erasing your ex's footprint in your life? If you choose to keep them, make sure that they don't mess with your emotions. There's no point in preserving something that will keep on reminding you of the fights, endless arguments, and bad times you had with your ex.

Erasing photos of your ex is your choice. Never let anyone compel you to delete or keep them. No one should judge you on how you decide to get over a breakup. It is your life and your relationship. They are your photos, and you can choose what to do with them. Deleting those photographs doesn't make you cruel, just as keeping them does not imply that you're still hung up on your ex-partner.

There are many possibilities and varied thought processes that go into that choice. Some people delete some photos and keep others. Many psychologists recommend deleting your ex's photos, and for good reasons. These include;

First, it allows you to move on faster. Deleting the photographs erases the physical evidence of an event that hurt you. Essentially, it's the same as discarding your smartphone background image and taking down all photos of your ex-partner from your work desk and shelves. Your relationship ended. Erasing the photographs associated with that union takes away the reminders. It's a visual fresh start.

Also, it sends a clear message to your family and friends. Though this isn't the healthiest reason to delete the photographs of your ex, it's important. You don't want your loved ones to get the wrong message every time they see photos of you and your ex kissing and hugging. Deleting those photos lets your friends and relatives know that the relationship ended.

Sometimes, clearing photos of your ex from your social media timelines could hurt their feelings and create drama. Your ex might ask why you did so and spark an argument. But worrying about his or her feelings isn't your concern. Don't be afraid of doing something that will erase the memories of a relationship that hurt you.

It's time – delete your ex's number

You have come too far to turn back. You have taken a few disengagement steps, and it's time you make a significant cut. Just rip the bandaid off. After all, you have a better life to live, and your ex-partner doesn't have to be part of it. It's a bold move. Just delete his or her number and get ready to face each new day without them.

Don't ask what could have been

The truth is, what could have been isn't going to happen. Perhaps you have been dreaming up scenarios in your mind of exciting possibilities had the relationship worked. But your lives have taken the opposite directions. Let's be honest, thinking along these scenarios will distract you from the hardships you're facing. The thoughts will change nothing. Instead, they will reignite regrets, sadness, and other weird emotions.

Nothing is left to figure out

Your relationship is now in your past. There is nothing left to talk about. Why do you need his or her number? Wash your hands of him or her for your sanity. It is in your best interest to accept that it's over and get on with your life.

Your ex isn't worth pining over

Time is the most precious, but also most limited, resource in one's life. So, why waste it on someone who no longer has value to you or values you? Think about other important issues you should be handling instead of dragging around your ex and your broken relationship. You have so much potential to do amazing things. So don't let your ex keep you from achieving that.

Don't torture yourself with memories

Leave your past in the past. Having your ex's phone number reminds you of the time you had together. This will make your healing process more challenging. Please don't do that to yourself. Maybe you guys have had great times together, but there's a reason the union didn't work. If you choose to move on, just delete their number.

The point is, there is nothing more freeing than disengaging and getting over a breakup. Sure, you will never relive those good or bad times. You might feel nostalgic at some point, but there is so much more to live for now. It's time to get rid of the stuff that reignites old memories, delete your ex's number, and keep moving forward.

The no-contact rules are an effective strategy that can help you detox after a breakup. It's quite straightforward if you don't want your ex back, you now know how to end communication with them safely.

Step 2: Plan

Getting over a breakup is a big goal. It can be broken down into small milestones. Each of these milestones requires time and effort.

For instance, disengagement is a process, and once you complete it successfully, you will be one step closer to your bigger goal. Each day, you must ask yourself, *"What do I need to do today to achieve my objective?"* This question is at the heart of effective planning.

You have spent some time taking all the necessary steps to disengage from your ex and the relationship. Perhaps you have set disengagement goals and other objectives in the process of getting over your breakup. Having clearly defined objectives leads to being deliberate in planning how you will spend your time.

What are your priorities?

Thinking about your targets gets you started. It's also essential to think about your priorities. The term priorities refers to how important an issue, event, or subject is. Revisit your list of goals and set your priorities.

This is easier said than done. You must push yourself out of bed, get over that nagging feeling of missing your ex, and start knocking out your objectives one by one. For instance, you should get enough time to spend with your loved ones. These are people who will make you feel better and probably help you achieve your goal – staying happy after a messy end to your relationship.

Make a checklist of your daily tasks, no matter how minor they seem. Get started as soon as you can, as this will help you stay in control. The chances are that you will feel great satisfaction when you start crossing off items on your to-do list. These tasks may not be directly related to your previous relationship, but the sense of achievement will create a positive feeling that will counter any traces of negative thoughts.

Assess how you use your time. How do you spend your days? As mentioned earlier, watching TV shows and munching on junk all day long will not make things easier. Record what you do each day for a week. Add all that up. Have you allocated enough time for your official duties? Do you have some time to catch up with friends? Do you have enough time to rest? Answering these questions helps you understand how you spend your day and the areas that you should work on or dedicate more time to.

Now that you know your priorities and what you should be spending your precious time on, work on creating a daily schedule. Already you know your ex isn't a priority, so you will not have to plan weekly dates with him or her. If you used to spend weekends with your ex-partner, you could allocate that time to group workouts or picnics with your loved ones.

Planning your day gives you a shot to orchestrate a perfect day. Certain activities in your day like appointments are pre-determined. However, other tasks are not predetermined, and you can design them as you choose. Getting your tasks done on time will keep you motivated, even when going through a hard time.

Step 3: Unleash those endorphins

When reeling from a breakup, perhaps the last thing you want to do is go on a morning run or hit the gym. But it's not recommended to wallow in your misery or turn to stress eating. This downward spiral is bad news.

Sure, a breakup is never easy. But you shouldn't fall prey to the post-breakup spiral. Ditch that pint of ice cream and gain control of your physical fitness. This is one of the best ways to get over a breakup and move on gracefully.

What are endorphins?

Have you ever felt amazing after a hard workout? You have probably heard that the "high" feeling is caused by endorphins. These are tiny neurochemicals released by your body. They make you feel more confident and happier.

The term endorphin is a combination of two words – endogenous and morphine. Endogenous means *"from within,"* and the term *"morphine"* which is a pain reliever. Endorphins are naturally occurring in the brain and work like morphine. That means endorphins are natural pain relievers within your body.

Endorphins consist of larger group peptides and are produced by your body's central nervous system. They act on the opiate receptors in a human brain to reduce pain and increase pleasure. This creates the good or *"high"* feeling whenever you unleash these neurochemicals. Generally, your body releases endorphins in response to stress or pain. They are also released during other activities such as sex, eating, and intense workouts.

After a breakup, find ways to get your endorphins flowing. This can make you feel whole again. Running is one of the best ways to trigger the release of endorphins. There are other activities that can help you improve your mood and increase the impact of endorphins in your body. These activities include;

- Yoga

- Cycling

- Tai Chi

- Swimming

- Active sports such as boxing, basketball, soccer, and more

- Massage and meditation

The purpose of endorphins

As mentioned earlier, endorphins play many roles in the human body. The most common roles include reducing pain and increasing pleasure. These neurochemicals are involved in your body's natural reward circuits. They keep your body functioning even when you are stressed or injured.

Human beings are social beings. They thrive in communities. A growing amount of scientific evidence shows that endorphins can help reinforce social attachments. Though this may not be true today, in early human history, individuals who stuck in small social groups had a better chance of survival and reproduction.

Benefits of endorphins

These neurochemicals promote an overall sense of well-being and have many benefits. These include;

Alleviating depression: Recent studies show that nearly one in every five people will experience depression once during their lifetime. Other studies have analyzed the role of physical activity in alleviating the symptoms associated with depression. Most of these studies have established a positive link between workouts and the easing of depression.

Also, endorphins help reduce anxiety and stress. As breakups are associated with heightened levels of anxiety and stress, it is recommended to follow a workout program that triggers the release of endorphins. This can help you feel better even when going through hard times.

Boost your self-esteem: The positive feeling associated with endorphins can make you feel optimistic and more confident. This will boost your overall self-esteem. Breakups are associated with so much negativity that could lower your self-esteem. This is particularly true if you and your ex-partner had endless squabbles, and he or she said downgrading things to you. You need more endorphins to continue feeling better and overcome low self-esteem issues.

You may not know everything about endorphins, but it's evident that these amazing neuropeptides have a positive impact on your body. So, if you and your partner broke up recently, find ways to unleash them. They will make you feel better.

Breakups are always hard because they are connected to the confusing emotions of hurt and loss. Follow these steps of breakup detox and, in the end, you will feel better. Besides, you will gain clarity about what happened and the ability to move on faster. In the next chapter, you will learn how to protect yourself from *"social media backlash"* after a breakup.

Chapter Three: Protecting Yourself With Social Media

The evolution of Facebook, Instagram, Twitter, and other social media platforms have altered the way people perceive relationships. These platforms have become a prominent place to meet and connect with people on a global scale. Also, they are popular sites where lovers display their romantic unions to their peers.

In today's largely virtual world, there are countless ways to connect and communicate with other people. FaceTime, text messages, social media networks, and emails are some of the most popular ways to connect with your partner and peers.

Facebook is the most popular social media platform, with 1.69 billion users as of November 2019. The platform was created in 2014 with the aim of connecting people. Users can upload pictures, videos, and share their interests on Facebook. Over the past few years, this social media giant has become a reliable business arena for entrepreneurs.

Instagram, Twitter, and other social networks can facilitate and maintain healthy relationships between romantic partners. For example, you can view your partner's profile, link your profile to your partner's profile, view their pictures, and react to their posts.

The real problem with the use of social media after a breakup

Offline, breakups can range from awkward to awful, and they inspire a gamut of weird emotions for your ex and their close friends and relatives. These negative feelings usually fade as ex-partners grow apart, both physically and emotionally.

The advent of social media has complicated this process. It's nearly impossible to do anything privately today. Almost everything can be caught on camera and *"go viral"* on social media within a few hours. With that in mind, breakups and the healing process carry a heavier and more transparent burden, because so much of it is documented on social media.

Take the case of the legendary John Cena, a famous actor, rapper, and wrestler. He was spotted holding hands with an unknown woman a few days after Nikki Bella, his ex-girlfriend, announced that she was in love with Artem Chigvintsev. This drama played out on news platforms, blogs, social media, and other platforms on the internet.

Sometimes, the partner left behind may not be ready to move on. However, the moment they see their ex-partner out there with someone else, they feel motivated to put themselves out there. Is this the right thing to do? Is using social media a good decision when trying to get over a breakup?

Your friends and family will advise you to unfollow or even block your ex on social media. Unfortunately, these platforms are likely to serve you a dose of reminders of your past relationships due to their advanced algorithms. These reminders make it more challenging for you to get over an old flame.

For example, Facebook has done an excellent job in creating an outstanding experience for its users. Some features such as the *"News Feed"* show you the specific *"stories that matter most,"* based on an advanced algorithm that includes the nature of the content you post and previous interactions you have had with different posts.

"Memories" or *"On this Day"* is another feature that shows your interactions or pictures that you shared a year or several years ago on the same day. Also, Facebook has the *"Friend Suggestions"* feature

that allows you to automatically see posts from your mutual friends where you can view comments from someone you already blocked.

These are just a few examples of upsetting encounters that can occur on social media that make breakups even more difficult. The real problem with Facebook and other social networks' algorithms is that they don't understand the complicated social data as a human would. Even after you block or unfriend your ex, the unpredictable outcomes of these algorithms can create upsetting experiences for users going through a breakup.

Seeing your ex's posts with a new lover often stings. It can push you to actively seek social interactions with just about anyone in an effort to spark jealousy, counter the loneliness, or reject your feelings. It can also be tempting to document what you do and share it on social media for everyone to see, particularly your ex. The content you share will give your ex a silent confirmation about how you are faring after the split.

If you are still grieving the loss of your ex, sharing a happy face on social media may be a way to show everyone that you feel better. It is a way to paint a picture in which you seem to have moved on, you're no longer crying, but rather moving toward a brighter future. Whether you are lounging by a pool, at a rooftop party, or an actual date, the picture you paint on social media announces that you're carrying on, and perhaps your life is even better without your ex.

Perhaps you are truly over the breakup. Or perhaps you are just faking it, and you would rather be home sleeping or watching your favorite TV show. So, is it recommended to publicly present your personal life to show your ex that you have moved on? Could this strategy backfire and hurt you more? To what extent should you use social media after a breakup?

When you fall in love and start a new relationship, you may have introduced your lover on social networks. In most cases, this legitimizes the union in the eyes of fans, followers, and friends. When things don't work out as you expected, and the relationship comes to an end, there is no clear way to let your social media connections know about the breakup.

Some people choose to delete all traces of their ex and broadcast the breakup to everyone. Others leave their social media posts untouched and never announce their breakups. Some social media users disclose their relationship hardships and breakups with varying levels of information about why the union ended.

This strategy gets details about your breakup out quickly. It is a choice with many disadvantages. First, it lets your connections (and your ex's connections) into your love life. No matter how wisely you craft your captions, the post will attract countless opinions, both positive and negative. Are you ready to handle the negative opinions?

Not every relationship has a happy ending. If you are going through a breakup, be careful when using social media. You may be looking for instant gratification and decide to let off steam and vent about your ex-partner. This is a choice you may come to regret later. Stay calm, and think rationally about whether to take the breakup to social media.

Practice "social media distancing"

There are many factors that you must analyze to determine whether you should continue using social media, unfollow your ex, or just avoid social media altogether. If you've always had a substantial social media presence, you may not want to change anything just because you're going through a breakup. Even if you have lost your lover, you don't have to lose your current connection to the world.

Actually, using social media wisely will keep things feeling normal and create a sense of normalcy in your life as you heal.

However, if you feel the pressure to *"put on a happy face,"* you should stop. The pressure to maintain a certain image because you want to prove something to your ex might make you feel overwhelmed by the breakup and social media. In that case, it's best to take the time to think through your options.

Putting a fictional story on social media that looks like a fairy tale makes actually achieving it more elusive. In the end, you will get the opposite effect of everything you wished to accomplish. This will send you further into despair instead of pulling you out of the pain of a breakup.

Remember, different severed relationships call for different actions. It's essential to be honest with yourself. Do your ex's posts on social media bother you? If not, you don't have to do anything. Listen to your emotions, and do what's best for your heart.

When to unfollow, mute, and unfriend your ex-partner

Depending on how bad the breakup is, you may want to mute, unfriend, or unfollow your ex on social networks for a few months. The period of *"social media distancing"* depends on how you feel whenever you see their posts on social media. If you have many mutual friends with your ex-lover, unfollow or unfriend them too, to avoid bumping into your ex's posts through them.

When freshly heartbroken, distance is essential. Later, if your ex-lover is a legitimate friend, you can try to re-engage. However, when the heartache is still fresh, it's a good idea to just mute or unfollow them. This doesn't mean you shouldn't take the right steps to protect yourself. If you suspect your social media response is likely to be met negatively, let your ex know that you need some distance, not that you are trying to erase them from your life.

It's also recommended to disable *"TimeHop"* and *"On This Day"* features on Facebook. This will prevent some surprising memories of how happy you and your ex were from years before. On Twitter and Instagram, use the *"mute"* feature if you don't want to take more harsh action like *"unfollowing."*

Maintain the distance

Unfollowing or muting your ex won't stop you from stalking them. If you're afraid that you will snoop into your ex-partner's social media profiles, you may want to modify your browser to reroute the URL of your ex's social media profiles to another page. For example, you can reroute it to a Google Doc with all the reasons you shouldn't be contacting that person.

On mobile, the most effective way to stop obsessively stalking your ex-partner is blocking them. If your ex has set their profiles as *"public,"* you can still see them whenever you are logged in to your account. In that case, it's best to block them.

Blocking someone on social media is a harsh action. If you are worried about burning bridges, tell your ex that you intend to block them. Be honest with your ex and let them know that your action is not personal or vindictive. Instead, these measures are for your emotional survival and the need for privacy and separation.

You will benefit from keeping both physical and social media distance after a nasty breakup. Indeed, the ways you will benefit from avoiding your ex-partner on social networks go deeper than you think. For many people, breaking up needs some space. Though you might feel a sigh of relief every time you view your ex's posts, that might result in having awful feelings in the long-run. It would be best to take some time away from various things that remind you of a past relationship and begin creating the *"new normal."* Remember, your new normal should not be defined by your past relationship.

Perhaps you feel that you are addicted to your ex-partner. Do you find yourself constantly checking your phone to find out whether your ex has sent a text message or commented on your recent post? If this is the position you find yourself in, it is in your best interest to be open to learning what's happening to you psychologically, and figure out why you are feeling this way. For instance, figure out why you cannot keep your eyes off your ex's social media and how you feel about it.

When to block your ex

I spoke with many people while doing research for this book, and the majority preferred or recommended full-on blocking an ex-partner. This will prevent them from seeing the content you post and also prevent you from stalking your ex when you begin feeling sad or nostalgic. Another advantage of blocking your ex is that his or her comments or replies on posts will be hidden.

Don't just unfriend your ex. This is important, particularly when you think that you can be a *"tourist"* in their life every time you log in to social media. Though this doesn't mean that you can never be friends on social media, you need emotional and physical distance to heal after the split.

What about relatives?

Your ex's relatives and friends might try to post negative comments on social media. Again, how you handle this issue depends on how you feel about the content they post. If, for example, your ex's Uncle Ryan's bedazzled fanny packs on Instagram don't upset you, you don't need to block or unfollow him. But if seeing your ex's sister's posts hit too close to home, it's best to take the right precautions to stay sane and happy.

Some friends and relatives might find that you unfriended them and may even ask about it. Just tell them the version that you told your ex – you are only taking the space you need. Other friends and relatives rarely get involved in other people's matters and may not notice that you unfollowed your ex or ask about the breakup.

What's okay to post?

Is it a good idea to react to posts by an ex?

This is a common question among people going through a breakup, and the answer depends on why you would want to react to your ex's posts. If you like their posts because you're on good terms and you don't feel any lingering romantic attachment, there's no problem with that. However, it's still a good idea to save the reactions for major life events.

Perhaps you had a strong friendship before you started dating. It is easy to break up and still maintain a friendship with social media. Otherwise, you should keep a little bit of emotional and social media distance. The point is, he or she is an ex for a reason. So keep a little distance to avoid blowing up your recovery process after a breakup.

Even if you have managed to get over the relationship, don't assume your ex is on the same page. By reacting to their posts on social media, you are sending a message or expectation of the possibility of reconciling. If you hurt them, it might feel painful or overwhelming for them to have you liking their content on social media, particularly when you are no longer in their life.

How about posting about your breakup on social media? Absolutely not! It is simply self-indulgent. According to most psychologists, there's something narcissistic in thinking that everyone or the world cares[2]. People who are already in your life and care about you will know about the breakup, and that means posting about it isn't relevant.

Posts involving breakups often get overshared on social networks, and this is unnecessary. It's also disrespectful to your ex. It is inflammatory to discuss the severed relationship on social media. Generally, it is unfair on the other person, and a breakup shouldn't be discussed on social media. Just avoid posting it at all costs.

Should you consider a couple's breakup post?

Worded posts are something common in celebrity culture. Think about Chris and Gwyneth's genre-defining *"conscious uncoupling,"* and Jenna Dewan and Channing Tatum's more recent *"we've lovingly decided to separate."*

Unless you're a public figure or have an important brand to protect, avoid a couple's breakup posts. If you *must* do this kind of post, agree with your partner the specific words to be used. This will prevent instances of misinterpretation.

If you have nude photographs of your former partner, act wisely. Breakups often bring out the worst in people, especially when upset or humiliated. Holding on to those photographs can lead to behavior that you might regret for the rest of your life. All it may take is a few

---

[2] (2017, May 21). How Does a Narcissist Think? | Psychology Today. Retrieved July 22, 2020, from https://www.psychologytoday.com/us/blog/the-legacy-distorted-love/201705/how-does-narcissist-think

glasses of wine or a couple beers with your buddies for you to start using those photos to humiliate your former partner.

Disseminating such photographs counts as revenge porn, an offense that could send you to prison in some countries. Besides, you are not going to be single forever, and after some time, you will start dating again. Imagine how awkward it would be to have your new flame find nude photographs of your former partner. Just delete any such pictures, and let your ex know that you have deleted those images.

If you are in the same WhatsApp group with your ex and their friends, choose your path wisely. It can be brutal to spend time in such a group. Just drop a nice little message letting everyone know that you will be leaving the group, and it was nice hanging out with them. If you want to keep in touch with someone in that group, you can send a message to them individually.

Should you delete all your social media accounts?

You have probably discarded the physical things that remind you of your past relationship. His or her clothes, gifts, and other things that reignite the feelings of anger and pain of losing someone you cared about are no longer in your apartment. You also deleted the social media posts and unfollowed your ex, but he or she cannot stop finding ways to contact you on social media. What should you do? Block them or delete your social media accounts?

Deactivating or deleting social media accounts might set you free

Breakups, whether expected or unexpected, are hard. During these hard times, it is easy to submit to the unprecedented siren song of social media stalking and misbehavior. Unfortunately, what might feel good to you through the lens of a breakup might not be good for public consumption.

In the first section of this chapter, I wrote about the things you should and shouldn't do on social media after a breakup. But there is a good chance you are still checking what your ex is doing on social media, even after you unfollowed them. An alternative to the more soft actions of unfollowing your ex is to deactivate your social media accounts. Or you can have a trusted friend or relative change your account's passwords. Avoid looking back until you feel you're ready to start using social media again.

This move is everything you need to collect yourself and keep moving after a breakup. Best of all, deactivating your social media accounts leaves behind zero evidence for your followers to gawk at after the breakup dust clears. You will have enough time to heal because you will not bump into annoying comments from a friend or your ex's family.

Deactivating your social media accounts puts an end to all the post-breakup logistics. Do you keep following your ex's posts, and if so, do you really need to watch their story updates and like their recent pictures? Is it normal to take a picture of a tree and post it social media, or will you appear desperate if you post your recent pictures?

These are some of the tedious questions that you will have to deal with. They are all self-inflicted. One of the most effective ways to end any form of uncertainty (and wipe out your presence on social media) is to deactivate your social media accounts.

However, this strategy is linked to a big caveat. If your Facebook, Instagram, or other social media account is offering you some genuine sense of comfort and connection during this time of grief, don't delete it. Although I do think digital detox and wiping out all the posts that remind you of your ex could be helpful.

Most people don't realize how attached they have become to connecting with other people, or how much they rely on their contact with the world via social media. If you realize you cannot deactivate your social media accounts, take the right measures to protect yourself. For instance, you can block your ex, unfollow them, and unfollow all mutual friends. Be careful not to obsess over what your ex shares on social media.

If you told your psychologist that you were considering wiping out your social media presence, they would ask you how you feel when scrolling through your social media feed. Do you get excited by just seeing what your fans are up to? Do you see one of your favorite artists out at a concert and say, *"I haven't been to a concert in a while?"* Sometimes, social media can be motivating and inspiring. However, if you find social media more draining than motivating, just deactivate your social media accounts.

Have you ever realized that a heart-wrenching photo posted by your ex could affect you negatively? It can make you feel that everything you worked so hard to achieve is now gone. Perhaps you had moved on, but a single post could reignite the pain all over again! Most people are familiar with the twinge of pain and self-doubt that might ensue. Nothing could make you feel pathetic faster than the thought, *"What! They went out partying with **my** friends?"*

Spending too much time on your ex-partner's social media strengthens your fixation, which could prolong your healing process after a nasty breakup. It is still possible to lurk on your ex even if you are technically *"away"* from social media, but there is a huge difference between accidentally seeing something and intentionally scrolling and looking for something.

In the wake of an ended relationship, it's challenging to maintain a level head on social networks, let alone posting anything like *"good content"* on these platforms. The jilted lover might use social networks to peer into the other person's happy life like a voyeur. Or they can use these platforms to compulsively check on their ex as a proxy for preserving some kind of real-life connection.

On the other hand, the single, happy person might decide to take advantage of various social networks to fire off some *"thirsty"* images, post funny screenshots from dating apps, or overly perform and showcase just how great they're doing being single.

Generally, unplugging from social media ends the direct or indirect discussion about who is winning after the breakup. It squashes the urge to make posts that prove how cool or hot you are. This misguided impulse might leave you waiting for a simple *"reaction"* rather than delivering a blow to your ex-lover's psyche. Like it or not, it is very tempting to make posts intended to remind your ex that they were dating someone cool, hot, and has a New York Times subscription.

The point is, deactivating your social media accounts isn't some kind of silver bullet, but now you know the timeworn benefits of unplugging from social networks and focusing on other activities that could help you heal faster. Analyze all the necessary factors and make the right choice for you.

Chapter Four: Don't Rush Into The Dating Game Too Soon

The moment you find yourself ranting about your past relationship while on a date, is a clear sign that you still need some time. Meeting new people might be a good way to realize there are plenty of fish in the sea, but you don't want to be sobbing about your last relationship over drinks with someone new!

Wait a little while before you start dating again. Give yourself some time before you let another person take up space in your heart after a breakup. Even when a few weeks have passed since you were last in someone's arms and you feel like you need to be enraptured in one's chest... wait!

Perhaps you are wondering *why*.

You don't want to jump into dating too soon and end up shattered again. It's a double whammy. You will have double the pain to deal with, simply because you couldn't wait. So don't rush into seeing someone. Take care of yourself first, get over the former relationship, and when you're ready, you can start (successfully) dating again.

Most people need time to grieve after a heart-shattering breakup. But how will you know that the grieving time is over, you have fully healed, and you're ready to start dating again? No two people's timelines are the same. Besides, you can meet someone new at any time. This doesn't mean it is impossible to tell if you are rebounding. Luckily, you can keep on checking in with yourself about the entire healing process. Pay special attention to how you feel about the previous relation, the breakup, your ex, and life in general.

In the previous chapter, I explained various stages of grieving and acceptance. It takes time to understand what happened, to accept it, and to make peace with it. This takes a different amount of time for different people. Just because your friend was able to get over a breakup within two or three months, it doesn't mean you should get back to dating after two months! You should also be careful not to judge yourself if you think you are taking too long to bounce back from a breakup. Remember, being ready to start dating doesn't happen on a schedule.

Focus on keeping tabs on your emotions and how you are relating to other people around you. Work towards positioning yourself in a healthy *"starting a new path"* routine instead of rebounding. Wait until you feel strong and grounded before you jump into dating. However, if it's been more than six months or a year and you still feel messed up by your previous relationship, seek help. Talk to someone you trust. This could be a close relative, friend, or even a counselor. Unless you are ready, a new relationship is likely to do more harm than good.

A breakup is challenging, and it takes something from you. Dating someone immediately might feel like a solution for loneliness and inadequacy, but it's a dangerous path. So avoid it.

Dangers of dating *too* soon

Breakups are heart-wrenching experiences marked by unhappiness, distress, and sometimes even a loss of sense of self. Does seeking comfort in a new relationship help the healing process? Could it alleviate your pain and help you move on? Are the rebound relationships always doomed to be flings, or can they become stable, happy, and long-term relationships?

A rebound relationship is simply a romantic relationship that starts shortly after the end of a previous union. Most people prefer a rebound because it reduces their time of being single. Other people think that being with someone else will help them get over the broken relationship more easily. It's like they replace what they lost with something new. But is this the case?

Most marriage counselors and psychologists advise against rebound relationships, and for good reason. They are an indulgent distraction that will prevent you from dealing with what happened. Caring relatives and friends will tell you that a rebound relationship cuts short your time to evaluate yourself and what you need. Though it can make you feel good in the moment, you should think about its downsides.

All these concerns are valid. But are rebound relationships bad? Maybe not. If your goal is to move on, starting a new relationship can help. It can boost your self-esteem, particularly if the new partner is caring and respects you. Think about it, bonding with a new person might create attachment security – the habit of trusting, a feeling of safety, and comfort with intimacy.

Does this mean you can end a relationship today and start dating a few days later? Timing is key, and this is where most people make a big mistake. Here are the dangers of jumping into dating too soon after a severed relationship.

You end up crying in your wine

If you don't take time to grieve, process what you have been through, and take care of your emotions after a breakup, you will end up crying in your wine, probably during a date. Admit that you are trying to suppress sad thoughts associated with the loss you recently experienced. You might think that you are escaping the worst of these hurt feelings, but that may not be the case.

The chances are that these suppressed thoughts will catch up with you in the future. Perhaps you are a glass or two of wine into your date, and the thoughts of your past relationship hit you. The chances are that you won't be able to suppress your tears.

You complicate things by jumping into the bed with the "new someone"

I'm not judging anyone. You are obviously free to get intimate with whoever you choose, any time you want. But ensure that's actually what you have planned to do, not because feelings of loneliness and inadequacy are compelling you to do so. Your life is already in a complicated state, and you don't want to heap more regrets on yourself.

You do something for the wrong reasons

Why are you dating in the first place? Do you think jumping from one person's heart to another person's arms is the right move? Actually, this is an effective way of barring yourself from developing meaningful and deep relationships.

Or you are just keeping yourself from getting *"messed up"* again? Stop and think things through. Sometimes, we run for the wrong reason from the right people. If you just jump into another relationship immediately, you will not get time to consider the possibility of missing out on something important. Sure, breakups hurt, but they come with important life lessons. Pay attention to those positive details.

You will not get enough time to heal

Unless you take sufficient downtime between romantic relationships, you will not recover fully. Your cracked heart is likely to have a whole lot of trouble getting put back together. Jumping right into another relationship means you have moved on, and you will be stuffing down any feelings that come up. That's what you will call *"baggage!"* Everyone knows the dangers of taking baggage into a new relationship. Similarly, you already know that you should never take open wounds into new romantic relationships.

No matter how many people you date, they will not help you forget your ex

You are jumping from one person you loved into a new relationship with another person you don't truly love. It won't end well. No matter how beautiful or cute the new partner is, they will not be distracting enough for you to forget about your past experiences completely.

You might even be thinking about your ex-partner more than you would if you were doing other activities like spending time with your friends or playing sports. It's even more challenging to make this direct comparison when you try to move on too quickly.

Do you know what will happen? You will end up leading the new person on. Even when you are perfectly fine noting these comparisons in your head and listing everything you don't like about your new partner, they don't know it. They probably don't deserve that, and the chances are that you will end up leading them on.

When you get involved in another relationship too soon, you will most likely be disappointed. It is not possible to be completely sure if your heart has healed, and you cannot have an equally serious feeling for two people. You're angry about what happened in your past relationship, and now you are trying to be happy and love your new partner.

64

In case you are disappointed in your new relationship, it's possible to start rethinking your options about giving your ex a second chance. It's easy to start thinking that there is no better person for you out there. But there is – just spend enough time, clear your mind, and get ready for someone you can bond with very well.

Are you rushing into a relationship too soon?

You need sufficient time to process your breakup, no matter what caused it. Otherwise, you will experience the nasty issues I just discussed. It's not always easy to know when you are ready to start dating again. Here are the signs you should pay attention to and step back to evaluate your healing process.

You're going through bad motions with just anyone

Are you dating just to date, rather than feeling a strong bond between you and the other person? This is not a good sign for your relationship's future. Do you want a new person in your life, or you just need a distraction? If you cannot instantly list the virtues of the partner you need and align that list with someone you are considering letting in, take a step back. Don't date someone just because you want a relationship.

If the new relationship is going to be a distraction, that is a red flag that your very first post-split date will turn into a *"thing"* within a very short time. If you are currently dating the first person who showed interest in you, that's not a good sign, either.

If you want to start a meaningful and valuable romantic relationship, you must evaluate someone's core values and personality. If you realize you're likely to date the first attractive person who showed interest in you after a breakup, you are simply rushing into the dating game.

Well, if the good universe brought you the right person after an emotional split, no judgment. However, if you strongly feel that you can easily switch the new partner with another better person as if you are shuffling a deck of cards, something is wrong. It's time to reassess your situation, what you really want, and focus on getting over the emotional split you just had.

When was the last time you spent time with your friends?

If you cannot remember the last time you went out with your friends, you still need more time to figure out what you want. Do you still have friends you can talk to about the things happening to you? One of the common signs that things are happening too fast is the loss of friends. Losing good friends might mean that you are spending too much time with your new partner. Perhaps your best friends expressed concerns about your new relationship, and you decided to cut them out.

No matter what happened, you are now losing friends that were previously helpful and precious. This is a sign you are moving too fast, and you need to slow down. One beautiful thing about severed relationships is that they create more time and opportunities to spend with friends and relatives. If you have missed out on these opportunities, it's time to check in with yourself and evaluate everything. Find out if you are overlooking something, making a mistake, or if everything is happening as planned.

You are still keeping tabs your ex

Let's get a few things clear here. Dating a new person isn't bringing your ex back. And if you have read this book this far, you are not planning to get back together with them. It doesn't matter how attractive you find the new partner or what they think about your ex-partner. Keeping an eye on your previous lover is never a good idea.

Be careful if you still hope your ex will notice something new about you and express interest in you again. If part of your intention in a new relationship has something to do with your ex-partner, that's a sign you are not ready to start dating.

You need a romantic relationship that is all about you and a strong bond that you share with a person you love, not some kind of ghost in your previous relationship. Give yourself time to get over the issues of your previous relationship, and you will be ready to date for the right reason again soon.

You need someone to help you rediscover yourself

In the wake of an emotional split, you have the best chance to evaluate and redefine yourself. And I will give you a pro tip – it's better to go through this journey on your own, not at the whim of another person. Be very careful if you are looking for another person to define you. Get to know yourself before you get into a new relationship. This new version of you might be different from the version that was dating your ex-partner.

The point is, you must recover your unique sense of self. Sometimes, people leaving a long-term relationship find that it's like they no longer know themselves. Such people should spend sufficient time to rediscover who they are outside of a romantic relationship. This will help them understand who they have become before they start a new relationship.

Some of the exciting ways to redefine yourself include making new friends, trying new hobbies, and being more mindful. Knowing your true self and what you want will effectively prepare you for whatever love and life throws at you. If, deep down, you feel like you need someone to help you to redefine yourself, slow down. Don't jump back to the dating game yet.

You can't stand being single

Being single after a breakup can be scary, but at the same time, it can be liberating. If you're not giving yourself sufficient time to experience this, it's a good idea to check in with yourself and find out why you desire another relationship so soon.

If you really hate being single and have a history of avoiding being single (even if it means hooking up with people who are not good enough for you), take a step back. It appears your relationships are always rushed, including the one you have been thinking about lately. Remember, there is nothing wrong with being single. Actually, it gives you the opportunity to interpret issues from a new perspective and get more clarity on various aspects of your life.

It is a good idea to be purposely single. That means you are single because you choose to be single, not because no one is ready to date you. You can choose to be single for a month or even more after a relationship ends. This offers you sufficient time to get your head straight, understand yourself better, and focus on self-development. These are some of the things that can help make your next relationship better.

Within that time you choose to be single, you will actually master the art of being a single, happy person. You will no longer feel lonely or inadequate. Just focus on yourself and how you can become a better version of yourself. Remember, self-development doesn't mean you are correcting your inadequacies; it means simply doing things that are more satisfying to you. For example, you can spend more time with your friends, start a workout routine, or pick up a new hobby.

Are you in control of your relationship?

If you are not in control of your relationship, that's another warning sign that you are rushing into something. This sounds weird, but it might make sense if you think critically about it. One reliable way to tell if a relationship is right for you is to feel in control of what is happening, including the ability to terminate the relationship. Before you get back into the dating game, find out if you are confident enough to end a relationship.

This doesn't make you a pessimist, but it would be best if you were sure that in case the new relationship doesn't work as expected, you can trust yourself to end it before you get hurt once again. If you cannot make such a decision and implement it, it could be a sign that you are still clinging to a bad idea of always being in a romantic relationship, and you are afraid of being single.

Unless you are sure you'd be fine on your own (if a new relationship doesn't work out), it's best you start spending more time with your friends and loved ones, rather than jumping into dating too soon.

You are not ready, and you know it

There is a good chance that you have been thinking about your readiness to date. Whether you refer to yourself as a *"serial monogamist,"* think about it when with your new partner, or even crack jokes about it when with your friends, your inner feelings might be peeking out. If you pay attention to those feelings, you will know whether you are ready to get into a serious relationship. On the flip side, you will also know if you are not ready for a serious relationship.

Being single after a breakup can be challenging. It can be confusing if you are used to having someone you love in your life. However, giving yourself some time to heal, redefine yourself, and make some selfish decisions are important parts of getting over a breakup. You will be surprised when you learn how strong you have become.

Just slow down

We all know that breakups hurt. You now know the dangers of rushing into the dating game without taking enough time to heal. Most men and women aspire to be in a steady relationship or marriage, and being single for a long time may sound unbearable to them.

A new relationship might sound like an interesting idea within those first few weeks, particularly when endorphins are coursing from head to toe, and you just want to be with someone. This isn't the time to pay attention to that feeling of lightheadedness or romance. Apply the brakes and take it easy. You are definitely hurting from your recent split, and it's a bad idea to immediately jump into a new relationship.

So, how long should you wait?

Two weeks?

Six months?

A year?

There is no specific amount of time you are supposed to wait after an emotional split to date again. After my first romantic relationship ended, I didn't know how soon I would reactivate my OkCupid account, the platform where it all started. Some of my close friends said, *"You do not want to go on a date and come home crying that you wish you had your ex back!"*

When I relayed this to another friend, he said, *"It's fine to cry."* These attitudes reflect a widespread disagreement over how long one should wait before they start dating after a breakup. Some people still believe (to say it crudely) that the best way to get over an ex is to get under someone else. Others are adamant that it is unfair to the person you will be dating if you are not fully over the pain and loss of your previous relationship.

The point is, there's no right or wrong amount of time to wait before you get into a new relationship, because circumstances vary widely. Therefore, you should focus on yourself and the uniqueness of your situation. There are other important signs you should look out for to know whether you are ready to start dating again.

You have learned many things about yourself

There is no specific period within which you should grieve after a breakup. Similarly, there is no specific timeline when it comes to jumping back into dating. However, you should first work through your sadness and anger. Take a few weeks or a few months – focus on what feels right for you. Make it more about knowing yourself rather than counting the days you have been single after a disturbing emotional split.

You are human. And humans have the habit of spending a lot of time worrying about relationships with those around them. In reality, the single most important relationship that matters in life is the one you maintain with yourself. The only entity that travels with you and will stick around you for the rest of your life is *you*. Don't get this twisted; I'm just emphasizing the importance of knowing yourself and maintaining a good relationship with your inner self.

If you know yourself deeply, the bad, the ugly, and the good, you will find it easy to accept who you are. It can be quite challenging to accept some character traits that you perceive as negative, like laziness. If that's part of you, it's important to start honoring it instead of living in denial. Denying it doesn't make it go away. You can start by learning the benefits of laziness, enjoy it, and let it work in your favor. From this kind of self-love, you can nature, grow, develop, thrive, and even flourish.

Before you get into a new relationship, make sure you have learned a lot about yourself. Learn to accept who you are. This will make you more independent of the opinions of your relatives, friends, and other people. Focus on knowing what works for you and what's good for you. Everything else, from your ex and other people who might want to judge you, is irrelevant.

You're the expert of yourself. You're in charge of your personality and thoughts. Remember, self-awareness and independence are linked to higher levels of self-confidence. With knowledge comes confidence and reliable decision making. This is exactly what you need. You are going through a hard time, and you don't want to make mistakes that you will live to regret. There is no space for doubt once you know who you are and what you want.

You are now ready to be a reliable partner

Can you spot a happy relationship at a glance? While no one knows exactly what goes on between a couple, many decades of social science research into sex, love, and relationships have revealed that a number of behaviors can predict when a relationship is on solid ground or when it is experiencing turbulence. A good relationship takes commitment, forgiveness, trust, and respect to establish a strong bond with your partner.

You cannot bring your best self to a relationship if you are still focused on your recent breakup. So it's best to wait until you feel that you can be a good partner to someone before you start dating. First, do the inner work. Focus on healing yourself and forgive yourself for being in a relationship that didn't work. Also, forgive your ex for any disappointment they may have caused.

Your future relationship will be much better if you let go of resentments, old pain, anger, doubts, and hate. Romantic relationships are dynamic. They undergo continuous change, reflect current circumstances, and other ups and downs. If you find it more challenging to deal with these issues, seek help. You can talk to a friend you trust or meet with a therapist to help you assess and process what happened. That way you can let go of the issues that might affect your future relationships.

You have made peace with being single

Sometimes, you don't have to wait until you get over your ex to start dating again. As long as you are not acting on feelings for your ex, your split will not impede your future relationships. It is normal to have feelings for someone you have been with for quite some time. But are you ready to move past those feelings?

If you still feel that personal issues on your part contributed to the breakup, you should address those issues. Otherwise, the same issues could affect your new relationship. Some of those issues include codependency or getting involved with toxic people. Take the time to work on these inner wounds before you start dating again.

You are probably experiencing a strong desire to fill the void created by your ex-partner. Don't fall into this trap. Instead, focus on feeling complete within yourself before letting in another partner. You will know you can start dating again the moment you realize you are strong enough to be single. Focus on learning your strengths and what you can offer a new mate rather than looking for a person to make you happy or fill a void.

You are happy with yourself

Happiness is simply the overall experience of pleasure and meaning. However, neither *"meaning"* nor *"pleasure"* alone can describe the term *"happiness."* That means you need meaning to make sense of your purpose in life. Also, you need pleasure to get a sense of joy and overall well-being.

If you want to be happy with yourself, simply add meaning and pleasure to your life. This will create happiness in the short run and in the long run. A significant other tends to make us happy and feel better about ourselves. Does this kind of happiness last forever? The moment we break out of the honeymoon phase, our insecurities may start to flare up.

It is recommended to work on these insecurities while you are single because there is a good chance they will pop up in your new relationship. Only when you feel that you are happy with yourself while being single, can you think of a new relationship.

You envision a brighter future

If you have been thinking about your future without feeling like a huge piece of you is missing, that's a good sign. You probably had planned a family vacation with your ex or even thought about walking down the aisle. Then the worst happened! It is normal to feel that you lost a lot and start visualizing yourself going through such great events without your ex. Do you find it challenging to continue your life alone?

The end of a romantic relationship is a grieving process. An integral part of this process involves orienting yourself to a life without your ex-partner. The future will no longer be a blurry mess. You will not struggle to make peace with what happened. After all, the relationship didn't work, you got hurt, and that's okay.

You have done your math correctly

Most people who have gone through a breakup start seriously dating anywhere from seven months to twelve months after an emotional split. However, this period depends on how long the relationship lasted, the major cause of the breakup, and other factors. This is the primary reason you cannot be absolutely sure about where you fall on this spectrum.

There is nothing wrong with seeking a little outside guidance. But you should do the math. Take two to three months for each year you were together to process your loss, grieve, and put yourself together. Simply put, you need enough solo time to prepare yourself for the next relationship.

Though these calculations are not based on any scientific data, they are based on data from the hundreds of conversations I've had with people while researching this book. It is a reliable way to check in with yourself as you continue to heal and redefine yourself. If you were together with your ex-partner for five years, you should give yourself at least ten to fifteen months to heal and reassess your priorities. At that point, you can determine whether you are ready to date or if you still need more time.

An inner voice is asking you to try

If you ever hear a small soft voice in your head urging you to reactivate your account in a dating app or find yourself daydreaming about a new relationship, take that as a cue. There is a good chance you will have that nagging inner feeling, and you will know that you are ready to enter into a new relationship.

Pay attention to the source of this little voice. Does it stem from the notion that *"you are running out of time"* to find a mate, or perhaps it is from loneliness? If you want to start dating under these circumstances, things might not work out so well. Perhaps you will begin to know someone and then get a little hesitant as your old fears start popping up. This is a sign you need more time to get over a breakup.

On the contrary, if you want to date again because you have a strong feeling that you are ready to enter into a relationship, then it's time. Be sure to check in with yourself just to be sure you have healed from the pain associated with the severed relationship, and you are ready to let a new partner in.

You have improved your bad habits

The cause of the breakup or whose fault it was doesn't matter. The most important thing is to analyze the bad habits you brought to the table and start improving them. The sooner you become a better version of yourself (acceptance), the sooner you get over the breakup, and the earlier you will start a new, healthy relationship.

If some of your bad patterns and habits played a part in your relationship's downfall, it would be a perfect idea to work through those first. This way, you will avoid dragging messy issues from your past relationships to the new one.

You have accepted the breakup fully

It's amazing how long some people can hold on to the idea of getting their ex back or thinking that the separation was a fluke. If you are still waiting for your ex-partner to call, it's time to shift your attention to recovery options, like seeing a therapist. I am not saying that you are crazy. But it wouldn't hurt to get a little bit selfish and focus on yourself.

In Chapter 1, I discussed the power of acceptance and how to accept that the relationship is really over. Remember, acceptance doesn't mean that you must know why the union didn't work. Sometimes, you may not understand everything fully. Acceptance is all about finding a new way to make peace with what happened and being able to move forward. That means you are fine knowing that you will never hear from your ex again.

You don't compare other people to your ex

The moment you realize that you cannot hear what your new partner is saying because you are too busy comparing them to your ex-partner, please take a step back. You are not ready to start dating. Take some time off until you can appreciate someone for what they have to offer. If you cannot, it means you are still stuck in the past to appreciate your present.

Now you know the dangers of rushing into dating, how long you should wait before dating again, and how to know if you are ready to start dating.

Let's work on another aspect of getting over a breakup – building your self-esteem.

Chapter Five: Rebuild your Self-Esteem

"Believe in yourself."

This is a message we encounter on television shows, books, and superhero comics. We are told that it's possible to accomplish big goals if we truly believe in ourselves. Is that always the reality?

I'm not saying that you _shouldn't_ believe in yourself. Accepting yourself for who you are and believing in yourself are essential factors in relationships, success, and overall well-being. Self-esteem plays an integral role in living a happy life. It strengthens our ability to believe in ourselves and the motivation to execute what we plan. Eventually, we reach fulfillment as we navigate this complicated life with a positive attitude.

Scientific evidence suggests that self-esteem has a direct impact on our overall well-being. It's best to keep this fact in mind for both our sake and other people around us. It refers to your beliefs about your worth and value. It revolves around the specific feelings you experience and is associated with your sense of worthiness.

Self-esteem has been a hot topic in the psychology world for many decades. Even Freud, the founding father of psychology, has many theories about self-esteem at the core of his outstanding scholarly contributions. He made strides in explaining the concept of self-esteem – what it is, how it develops, and the unique factors that influence it. This topic is vast and can take various directions. I will focus on self-esteem in relation to getting over a breakup. Here are a few important aspects to understand before we dive into rebuilding your self-esteem in the wake of an emotional split.

Self-concept Vs. self-esteem

Self-concept refers to the perception you have of yourself. It's simply the answer to the question, *"Who am I?"* It's all about understanding your own tendencies, preferences, thoughts, skills, weaknesses, and hobbies.

Self-esteem isn't exactly your self-concept. However, it is an integral part of your self-concept.

Self-image vs. self-esteem

Another important concept that you should learn about is self-image. It is similar to your self-concept in that it's all about how you think about or see yourself. However, self-image can be based on either reality or inaccurate thoughts. Your self-image might be close to reality or just illusions. Note that it's not completely in line with the objective reality or how other people around you perceive you.

Self-worth vs. self-esteem

Self-worth is a similar concept to self-esteem. However, there is a small, but important, line of difference. Self-esteem refers to what you feel, think, and believe about yourself. On the other hand, self-worth refers to the widespread recognition that you are a valuable human being worthy of love.

Self-confidence vs. self-esteem

Self-confidence isn't self-esteem. The former is all about how much you trust yourself and your ability to deal with various challenges, solve your problems, and engage well with the outside world. Based on this description, self-confidence is based on external measures of success rather than internal measures that are known to contribute to one's self-esteem. You can have high self-confidence in a specific field and lack self-esteem – a healthy sense of your overall value.

Self-efficacy vs. self-esteem

Just like self-confidence, self-efficacy is linked to self-esteem, but not a proxy for self-esteem. It refers to a firm belief in your ability to succeed at specific tasks. For instance, you can have high self-efficacy in playing football but low self-efficacy in solving mathematics problems in class. That means self-efficacy is somewhat more specific and is based on your external success instead of self-worth.

Self-compassion Vs. self-esteem

The concept of self-compassion centers on how you relate to yourself rather than how you perceive or judge yourself. Being self-compassionate means that you are forgiving and kind to yourself. Indeed, you avoid being overly critical and harsh. Self-compassion can lead you to a healthy sense of self-esteem.

Understanding the difference between these concepts and how they contribute to your self-esteem is an integral step in building your self-esteem back up after a relationship ends.

A breakup distorts self-esteem

Romantic relationships alter how two people in love perceive themselves. The partners develop shared activities, friends, and even overlapping self-perception – an important aspect of self-esteem.

This intertwining may leave their self-concepts vulnerable to an unanticipated change in the wake of a breakup. Most people experience negative self-concept change and reduced self-perception clarity after a breakup. Reduced clarity is associated with emotional distress and low self-esteem.

Given the nature of interdependence that characterize most romantic relationships, a breakup is likely to evoke a change in how you think of yourself. After all, you are forced to face a new world without your partner and redefine who you are in the absence of your ex. This is a somewhat confusing phase of your life, and you must tread carefully.

The pain of a severed relationship is intense, particularly when you discover someone you loved so much no longer wants you and isn't coming back. Despair might lead you to believe that you are not good enough to enjoy enduring love and care. Yet every living breathing person is likely to face various forms of rejection. The bridge over these troubled times is your self-esteem and awareness that the feeling of hopelessness is temporary.

Relentless self-criticism will confuse you and prolong the grieving process. This is bad news for your self-esteem and overall well-being. Never let self-criticism hijack your healing process after a breakup. Feeling sad, angry, or confused while grieving the loss of a romantic relationship is normal. However, you are likely to experience a higher level of emotional distress if you continue blaming yourself for what happened. That nagging self-blame can grow into a deep seated feeling that you are worthless and cannot maintain a healthy relationship.

This gut-wrenching agony is so unbearable that you might, despite whatever happened, go to any length to get your ex-partner back. Some of these desperate attempts include doing anything to get your ex's attention, endeavoring to talk things out, and more. If you are in this situation, it means that your sense of self-worth is dependent on your relationship with your ex.

The loss of self-esteem is a highly disruptive aspect of an emotional split. When you continue criticizing yourself, you pile more fault on the existing fault until you can think of nothing else but your perceived inadequacies. You become so obsessed with self-blame and forego the process of processing what happened and moving on.

Prioritize your self-esteem after an emotional split

As mentioned in the previous chapters, thinking through the history of the former relationship is an effective way of learning how you can handle a future relationship better. If you can successfully grieve the loss without attacking yourself, the entire healing process will be faster and smoother. Besides, it will set you up for anything else that comes your way in life.

Pay attention to the nature of your thoughts. Are you thinking objectively, or are you attacking yourself? Many people experience a spiral of self-criticism when going through a divorce or a painful breakup. Here's how to prioritize your self-esteem even when going through these hard issues.

Think about who you are, outside this relationship

Do you feel like you lost yourself along the way with your previous partner? Think about who you were before you met this person. Also, consider the kind of person you want to be now that the relationship has ended. Fine-tuning your hobbies, interests, and friendships are a valuable way to streamline your healing process.

Use this painful ending of a relationship as a way to re-evaluate yourself and grow into the person you want to be. This will help you strengthen your self-esteem. On the other hand, relentless self-blame and criticism will siphon your energy and self-esteem. List all your interests and set both short-term and long-term goals. Where do you want to be in three months, six months, a year, or more? The path forward is more clear and easier to follow when you know who you are and what you want to achieve.

Are your expectations realistic?

Today's culture has promoted the idea that true love comes easily. If that isn't the case, most people blame themselves for not meeting what appears to be the *"recommended love standard"* that is so easy for others to achieve.

In an ideal world, relationships and marriages would work perfectly. However, we are in the real world, and breakups happen. They help us discover more and learn the important things we need in a romantic relationship. The expectation that we will nail it this time, without knowledge, is unrealistic and somewhat self-defeating. For most people, it takes several lost loves to find a trusted person who sticks. Every time you criticize yourself, consider the idea that you're not inherently flawed. In thinking so, however, it might set you up for unrealistic expectations that love must come easily.

Think about what you learned from your ex-partner

Every failed relationship is a unique opportunity to take stock of what we learn about ourselves. Take the time to analyze what you learned. This will help you to understand yourself better and probably find a more loving partner in the future.

Avoid going down a self-criticism spiral. Whether you chastise yourself for your appearance, personality, or other things, just stop it. The moment you become aware of the self-criticism spiral, pick up your journal, and start writing about what the broken relationship taught you in terms of improvement as a person. Don't focus on your flaws or weaknesses. Examples of the things you may want to improve could be your communication skills, building up interests, or various hobbies of your own. Don't focus on negative issues such as being too fat or too needy.

Why should you prioritize your self-esteem?

Our nervous system is wired to connect and need others. A rejection or breakup can be very painful because of the lost connection. It can make you feel that your entire life has been wrecked. In the worst-case scenario, you can find yourself questioning who you are, what you want, where you are in this world, and whether you still have any worth.

Perhaps you put a lot of yourself into a relationship. Over the years, it became a kind of pillar by which you define yourself. This is why breakups eat into one's self-esteem like a highly corrosive acid. When that pillar falls, your self-esteem shatters. As mentioned in the earlier chapters, you might struggle with the feeling of being unworthy or the major cause of the split.

This is a deep hole that you don't want to get lost in. That's the main reason you should prioritize your self-esteem. Otherwise, negative thoughts will creep in, and before you know it, you will be having an additional problem – low self-esteem.

Simply put, low self-esteem is often characterized by feeling bad about yourself and a general lack of confidence. People battling with low self-esteem feel incompetent, unlovable, and awkward. They tend to be hypersensitive and have a somewhat fragile sense of self that gets wounded easily. Additionally, people with low self-esteem are usually hyper-aware and hyper-vigilant to signs of inadequacy, rejection, and rebuff. They see disapproval and rejection, even when it isn't the case. The danger lurks in that these people will do something embarrassing, make costly mistakes, expose themselves to ridicule, use poor judgment, or behave contemptibly. You don't want to add this terrible burden on your already shattered heart.

Everyone's self-esteem is vulnerable to people who openly ridicule them, criticize them, or point out their weaknesses. Life, in all its variety, appears to pose an ongoing threat to one's self-esteem. But the greatest threat to your self-esteem lurks within you.

As an observer of your thoughts, feelings, and behavior, you register these unique phenomena in consciousness and pass judgment on them. That means you might be your most severe critic, berating yourself mercilessly when you find yourself making a mistake, forgetting what you must remember, losing your self-control, breaking your most sacred promises, or behaving in ways that you regret.

This harsh self-criticism contributes to a negative perception of yourself, and this behavior is linked to severe consequences. For instance, if you believe that other people don't like you, there is a good chance you will avoid interactions with other people, become more defensive in your interactions, or even lash out. You are going through a hard time after a breakup, and you don't have the time and energy to handle the consequences of low self-esteem.

The nature and level to which you interact with other people are greatly influenced by your self-perception, no matter the accuracy.

Indeed, your self-perception represents an important foundation on which your interpersonal behaviors rest. When you perceive yourself negatively, whether you label yourself as obnoxious, awkward, shy, or unlovable, it becomes more challenging to believe other people will see you in a positive light.

The point is, low self-esteem is associated with a life full of misery. Rebuilding and fortifying your self-esteem is an important step in your recovery journey after a painful breakup.

No matter how much you listen to *I Knew You Were Trouble* by Taylor Swift, the pain of a breakup can sometimes feel unbearable. Having a chapter like a romantic relationship close in your life isn't something you would ever want to experience. Experiencing this kind of loss can affect your health and self-esteem badly. Here is how to rebuild your self-esteem after an emotional split.

Dive into self-care

If you have ever flown on a jet, you have probably heard the safety instructions that are announced before the flight. The unforgettable part of the script says, *"In case of a sudden loss of cabin pressure, an oxygen mask will descend from the ceiling. Grab it and pull it over your face. In case you are traveling with kids, secure your mask before helping them."*

At first, these instructions sounded strange until I began to consider the logic behind them. Many kids lack mental awareness and the physical ability to wear a mask over their face. It is up to the adult to help their kids pull the mask over their face. If the adult doesn't affix his or her mask first, they might pass out from lightheadedness and won't help their kids.

The principle behind these preflight instructions applies to your physical and mental health after a breakup. Let's face it. You have a million tasks to handle. If you don't take care of yourself, will you maintain the energy required to get over a breakup and, at the same time, handle your responsibilities? Self-care is all about treating yourself with love, gratitude, and respect.

In the words of Abba, the famed 1980s band, *"A breakup is never easy, but I have to go."* These are the last words we all think of before an emotional split. Whether you are still single or already connecting with a new partner, the single most important relationship you will have for the rest of your life is the relationship with yourself. The *only* person who will be with you through thick and thin, and from the day you were born to the day you bid this planet goodbye, is **you**.

To get over a breakup, you must prioritize this unique relationship with yourself. And you can achieve this through effective self-care. Here are the three most important elements of self-care.

1. Love

How do you interpret love? What does it feel like? Comforting, safe, warm, or fuzzy? Whatever love feels like in your world, focus on doing things that make you feel loved. Treat your body carefully and with love. Take a warm bath, get a relaxing massage, light a sweet-scented candle, and relax with a glass of wine.

Buy yourself an amazing gift and tell yourself how beautiful and smart you are every morning. Eat chocolate, take a hike, and hang out with friends or relatives who accept you for who you are. The point is, learn to do all the things you would have done if you were in a relationship. Learn how to love yourself more than anyone else, not out of extreme selfishness, but because you deserve it.

2. Respect

Your body and mind together form a temple. If you are into yoga and meditation or read personal development books, you must have heard this theory. Now is the time to embrace these ancient words. The food you eat and the words you think feed your inner self. So choose your path wisely.

You wouldn't throw trash in a temple or demoralize a loved one, right? Similarly, you should choose what you eat wisely and avoid calling yourself negative things just because you are going through a hard time after a breakup. Treat your skin, bones, flesh, and inner self like the most respected temples or sacred places ever built.

Why?

Because your soul and body are sacred.

3. Unequivocal gratitude

Appreciate what you have – food to eat, clean water, and a functional roof over your head. Not everyone is so lucky as to have all these blessings. Breakups are painful, no doubt. But reminding yourself of what you have and being thankful for it is at the core of self-care. This can help you strengthen your self-compassion and positive feelings and thinking.

Healing after a breakup isn't linear. It will take you some time to accept it. After a month or more, you will realize that you no longer miss your ex. As time goes on, something might trigger you, turning you into a ball of tears once again. Grief comes in waves, and those waves keep coming. But they will get smaller with time.

Please be kind to yourself. Take the time to focus on you. Use this opportunity to build your self-esteem. If you feel that you cannot face this healing process, consult with an experienced therapist or a trusted person. Most importantly, believe in yourself. You can do this, even if you don't see it yet.

Focus on self-development

Humans always want to do better. Throughout history, the desire to do better has led to better chances of survival. This instinctive trait is perceived as the desire for self-development and can help you transform your current life into something better. Regardless of what you are pursuing, self-development is an important part of your happiness and positive progress in life.

From birth, the subconscious mind is constantly imprinted with different beliefs based on suggestions and experiences from people's lives, the internet, media, cultural values, and more. Some of these beliefs are empowering, and others are just crippling. The empowering beliefs generate positive feelings such as self-confidence that perpetuate accomplishment and exploration. On the other hand, crippling beliefs tend to generate fear and other self-sabotaging feelings.

The source of one's misery lies in their addiction to violence, fear, anger, dishonesty, self-pity, resentment, jealousy, or other toxic emotions. Some people are addicted to negativity and mistakenly believe that it's somehow selfish to seek prosperity. They constantly upset themselves by judging other people and circumstances as unjust, unfair, wrong, bad, unacceptable, or immoral.

It's important to mention that your thoughts are a form of energy. They don't just float around in your mind. Each action is preceded by a thought. Your thoughts are governed by a law of attraction that determines the nature of the energy you attract.

To understand this concept, think of an employee who complains vociferously about unfair policies, improper working conditions, incompetent management, and just about everything else. This person can incite negativity of other people within hearing distance. That negative energy will attract disgruntlement that will permeate the entire workplace like a noxious gas!

Self-development is a broad field that revolves around empowering your status, knowledge, health, character, and other aspects of your life through your own efforts. It is a quest to make yourself better in different facets of your life. It begins with self-awareness and your ability to transform your character and habits.

Suppose you could successfully use the energy that you squandered on negative emotions and invest it in thoughts of what you desire to see manifested in your new life after a breakup. Suppose you laid rightful claims to be healthy, successful, and happy. You would realize that your thoughts rhyme with what your heart desires. These thoughts would attract similar positive thoughts.

Positive people and circumstances would start to appear, and this is exactly what you need to rebuild your self-esteem. There is a good chance you will increasingly learn to trust your intuition to recognize various opportunities whenever they present themselves. You no longer need to hold on to the bad feelings associated with a breakup. Focus on self-development, and you will start feeling better about yourself.

It takes time to transform the character and other aspects of human life. Some beliefs are so deeply ingrained that they're very hard to even recognize. I urge you to believe in the gradual process of self-development and take baby steps. Here are some important self-development tips that you may want to implement in that process.

Focus on your passion

Generally, relationships are time consuming. The time you would spend writing, practicing an instrument, playing a sport, reading, traveling, or networking suddenly turns into time spent with your partner. It's easy to forget what brought you pleasure or drove you before you fell in love.

Now that the relationship has ended, this is your chance to remember what you are passionate about and reignite it. Trust me, this passion will lead you somewhere.

Keep a journal

Starting a journal is one of the best ways to learn more about yourself. After a breakup, it is normal to feel vulnerable. Turn your attention inward and focus on yourself. Write down your aspirations, thoughts, fears, and general observations of the world. This is a good way to understand your abilities and emotions.

Spend time with your friends

Be honest. Being in a relationship might have taken up a lot of your time, and you didn't have enough time for your family and friends. Don't hate yourself for it. It happens to nearly everyone. As I said, relationships require commitment and can be time consuming.

It is possible to spend too much of your time with your significant other. This can create a distance between you and friends, family, and other important people in your life. If you recently broke up with your partner, now you have a chance to reconnect with friends.

Being in the company of people who care about you promotes positivity. Eventually, this will boost your self-esteem.

Don't rely on people to cheer you up

If your friends and other people around you care about you, they will cheer you up, whether you depend on them or not. It is essential to learn how to stay happy and cheer yourself up, though. You shouldn't be that friend who disappeared when you fell in love and reappear as extremely needy after the relationship didn't work.

It is possible to use your own sadness to successfully reflect and relate to different people who are also going through challenging experiences. Focus on being an inspiration to other people. Practice acceptance and positivity.

Avoid stalking your ex-partner

Nothing good ever came from stalking. Trust me, it will only make you seem creepy and pitiful. Don't focus on what your ex is doing. Instead, get to know yourself better and pursue what you want in life.

Create a no-negativity zone

After a breakup, most people suffer a series of negative thought spirals. Self-doubt and other toxic emotions creep in. If you are going through such hard times, you already have enough problems to deal with. There is nothing that can hurt you more than surrounding yourself with negativity. It's possible to think that you have these emotions under control. However, external factors can create an unacceptable level of negativity and dampen your mood.

To rebuild and maintain high self-esteem, you need to avoid things that create negative energy. Work towards getting over each hurdle quickly and stay happy. Sometimes, unexpected situations can pop up if you are still surrounded by negativity. The good news is that you can still remain composed with a positive outlook and get through these situations unscathed. Here are some tips to help you create a no-negativity zone.

Practice gratitude

Gratitude can fortify your self-esteem and overall emotional well-being by positively transforming your inner energy and reinforcing positivity. If you shift your thoughts and focus on what you have and everything that makes you happy, your brain will learn to notice the abundance in life. This will make you more grateful and happier overall. Remember, expressing gratitude is a choice. You can exercise it at any time. The moment you begin feeling negative, just think of an achievement or something you are grateful for.

Practice forgiveness

This is an important step to avoid negativity. Eliminate old sentiments and forgive yourself and others. Holding onto a grudge can block your ability to appreciate yourself and other people around you. Once you release the anger in your heart, you will be able to receive love from people who care about you and, in turn, give love to people you care about. Forgiveness creates more room in your heart for love. Eventually, this will improve your self-esteem.

Live for the moment

Negativity creeps in when you start ruminating about the cause of the breakup and worrying whether you will ever find true love. In the present moment, you are fine. You are probably not crying, and you no longer miss your ex. That's what matters, so focus on the moment.

Just ask yourself, *"what's true at this moment?"* You are alive, you have a roof over your head, you have friends who care about you, and most importantly, you have a source of income. Focusing on positive things will give you a sense of peace and joy. Move past negativity and be thankful for the things that you can enjoy at the moment.

Do things that make you happy

Are you doing something that's putting you in a weird mood or tearing you down? Just stop. Do something else that seems less of a chore, but a privilege. Acting in a positive way and doing things that you truly love can help break a negative mood. Afterward, you will feel happier and energized.

Stick to a work schedule with breaks

Schedule *"happy breaks,"* even when you have a very busy day. This is a great way to rejuvenate yourself and stay positive. The moment negativity strikes, you will be in a better position to avoid rumination. This is because you will have a positive activity approaching (during your happy break) to clear your mind. Taking care of yourself and focusing on positive habits will help you stay positive.

Go outside

Take a walk outside. This will boost blood circulation, bring fresh oxygen to your lungs, and clear your mind of toxic thoughts. Connecting with nature can make you happier and more rooted in your life. These are all elements of a non-negative zone. So, the next time you get upset, just take a walk outside and get fresh air.

Get a little sweaty

Regular exercise can make you happier, energized, and more productive. The positive impact of physical activity can last for many hours after your workout session. Unleashing endorphins can enhance your mood and break tension associated with negativity. Besides, physical exercise will help you stay in shape. That way, you will start feeling better about yourself.

Visualize your next adventure

In life, success starts with a goal. This goal could be quitting a bad habit, losing weight, or launching a business. Whether short-term or long-term, targets give us a purpose. They keep us headed in a specific direction, just like a compass. Of course, we all need hard work and determination to achieve these goals.

Aristotle simplified this process more than 2000 years ago. He described a few simple steps. First, set definite, clear, and practical goals. Secondly, have the right means to conquer each target or goal. The necessary means include materials, knowledge, methods, and money. Third, adjust your means to ensure that you achieve the goals you set in step one.

After a breakup, someone might feel disoriented and confused. But this shouldn't stop you from setting important goals in life. Even if you feel stuck, if you can start out with the right intentions and plan effectively, you can implement your plans effectively. Be sure to break the long-term goals into small daily or weekly ones. Conquer each goal at a time. These small wins will keep you motivated to stay on course. Besides, the sense of achievement will help boost your self-esteem.

Seeing is believing

Before you can believe in a target, you must get an idea of what the goal looks like. This is the reason visualization is important. Visualization involves creating a mental picture of a future event. The event represents the desired outcome, and having such a picture in your mind helps you to see the possibility of achieving a certain goal.

Through effective visualization, you can get a glimpse of your preferred future. For instance, you can visualize a happy holiday without your ex or a successful career without their help. When you get this image in your mind, you will be motivated to pursue that goal.

Don't confuse visualization with the common phrase going around – *"think it and you will become it."* That's neither a gimmick, nor does it compel you to hope or dream for a brighter future. Instead, visualization is a unique method of improving performance. It is supported by scientific evidence.

Think about athletes. Studies reveal that visualization increases their performance by boosting their concentration, coordination, and motivation. Also, it helps them to relax and reduce fear and anxiety. One researcher said, *"Visualization helps most athletes to execute their plan with poise, perfection, and confidence."*

Does visualization work?

Popular books such as *The Secret* assert that visualization is the secret to happiness and success. Believe it or not, your thoughts have power. If you can picture yourself staying on course and achieving your goals, those things are more likely to stick in your mind and keep you motivated to do the right thing. This is different from the common belief that you can manifest a Bugatti in your garage by thinking about owning one.

When you feel bored at work, what do you do? I used to do something weird. One day I decided to pass the time thinking of devouring a pint of delicious Cherry Garcia ice cream. The second I got a lunch break, I bought a pint of ice cream and ended up eating it in one sitting.

Our brain has been evolving for hundreds of thousands of years. Nothing a human brain does is purposeless or random. Visualization primes your mind to take a specific action. It tells your subconscious mind to work out a strategy to get what you are visualizing. This creates a kind of force to acquire the things you desire.

More than just a thought

Visualization is a dedicated practice, just like meditation. It involves creating a vivid image of your desired future and getting what you want in life. Visualization influences how you feel. It has to break through to your subconscious mind. At the end of a successful visualization session, you will feel motivated, energized, and positive.

Scientific evidence has revealed that a visualization is an indispensable tool for self-development. Even the greatest performers in history claim visualization contributed to their success. Learn how to visualize what you want, create a strategy to achieve it, and implement that strategy. Staying focused and making progress in whatever you do will keep you motivated. This is an important milestone in your quest to rebuild your self-esteem after a breakup.

Remind yourself how amazing you are

Everyone's self-esteem fluctuates and takes a major dip when one is going through a stressful life event like a breakup. But you are special in many ways. You deserve admiration, attention, success, recognition, and love. These are the things you want, but you are probably too afraid to admit.

Allowing yourself to acquire or believe that you deserve good things doesn't make you selfish. You are just a normal person who desires to have normal feelings and possessions like everyone else. Here are ways to remind yourself that you are an amazing person.

Connect with nature

For centuries, humans have found that reconnecting with nature is good for the body and mind. From rites of passage deep in the wild to today's East Asian culture that supports forest baths, humans have always perceived nature as an avenue for personal growth and healing.

There is something about connecting with nature that helps put issues in perspective. Getting off of your couch and enjoying the outdoor environment makes it easier for you to be mindfully present. It gives you the chance to clear your mind and toss aside issues that are not serving your interests. If you are feeling overwhelmed and need some time to remind yourself how good you are, go for a walk, bike ride, run, or sit on a park bench. Pay attention to the natural beauty that surrounds you.

Another way to connect with nature is by gazing at the clouds and stars. It is a powerful tool that helps humans transcend space-time reality. Most ancient civilizations looked to the sky and stars for power and guidance. Humans are made up of stardust and watching these amazing twinkling stars takes us beyond the mundane, into some kind of supreme consciousness. When I was a child, I used to stare at the stars. And it was fun.

Lend a hand

Helping other people is a fundamental part of humanity and creates an opportunity to bond together. In times of tragedy, you have heard those inspiring stories of people who helped others. Some people have played significant roles in helping others recover after natural disasters and terrorist attacks. You don't have to wait until a disaster occurs to help someone. You can lend a hand in many ways every day. Here's why helping others helps you as well.

First, doing something good makes you feel good. There is a good chance you will feel some sense of achievement. Seeing that smile or even tears of joy will be well worth it. Perhaps you did something simple for someone. Seeing them happy will remind you how good you are.

Other people will also notice that you are doing something good. Even if this isn't the reason you chose to help out, someone will be watching and appreciate your good deed. Even a simple gesture of kindness can make an outstanding impression.

Everyone has their own struggles

Perhaps you already know that everyone has their own struggles. But you haven't internalized this fact. Surround yourself with people who appreciate you and lift you up. This will make you feel safe and free to talk about your struggles with the people you trust.

This will open the door for the people close to you to talk about their self-worth and struggles. Being with people with whom you share struggles and strengths will make you feel less alone. Also, it can make your self-worth soar by simply helping others get through hard times.

The key to rebuilding your self-esteem after a breakup is to focus on yourself. Define your personal success and consistently work to make it a reality. With time, you will regain high self-esteem from self-care, a well-designed self-development plan, creating a no-negative zone, visualizing your future, and continually reminding yourself how amazing you are.

Remember, rebuilding your self-esteem isn't the end of your journey to get over a breakup. There are other important steps that you must take. Knowing what to do makes it possible to become better and happier. There are things that can cancel everything you have been doing to get over a breakup. The next chapter is all about the dos and don'ts after an emotional split.

Chapter Six: The Dos and Don'ts After a Breakup

Romantic relationships are a complicated part of human life. In some situations, it might be easy to know whether your romance will develop a lifelong union, or if the bond will snap within a few weeks. But this isn't always the case. Sometimes, people don't notice any signs of an inevitable emotional breakup. The latter hurts so much more.

Whether you saw it coming or it caught you by surprise, the pain of a breakup is inevitable. What matters is how you handle it. This is, by far, the most challenging quest. In the previous chapters, I described various processes intended to make you feel better about yourself. However, there are some small actions or choices that could mean the difference between fast healing and battling with the pain of a breakup for years. For example, one of those minor choices is getting a breakup haircut. Is it necessary? How will it impact your journey to getting over a breakup?

Actions have consequences

Everything you think, say, and do has consequences for yourself and other people in your life. Like a ripple in a pool, your actions spread out and affect everyone – you, your friends, relatives, and others. Everything is interconnected.

Consequences are the meeting point of your thoughts and reality. You cannot always foresee them, and trying to be 100 percent sure that you are doing everything perfectly might lead to indecisiveness and anxiety. Does this make getting over a breakup more complicated? Not really. You can resolve to do things that lead to

103

happiness, not sadness. Make choices that make you feel better about yourself, make you feel safe, and that promote unity.

Your intention is the key. Do you want to be hurtful or do you want to be helpful? If you feel that you are connected to your relatives, friends, and colleagues, you probably do not want to hurt them. The feeling of interconnectedness makes one sensitive to how their choices might affect other people. On the other hand, hatred might compel you to seek revenge on your ex. This is bad news.

Post-breakup actions with severe consequences

Sure, breakups are associated with extreme emotions and can mess up your decision-making ability. But none of these arguments can hold up in a court of law if you ever do anything destructive and find yourself in legal trouble. *"Sorry officer, I suffered an emotional breakdown."* This statement can't get you out of fines or imprisonment for aggressive behavior or other illegal activities.

The judge may take pity on you because they know a thing or two about an emotional split, but they will not let you off the hook for something sinister. An essential part of being an adult is not letting your emotions get the best of you. Gain control over your feelings before you do something with severe and lifelong consequences. Here are a few post-breakup choices I've seen with serious repercussions.

Defaming your ex-partner

Defamation is an action for which your ex-partner can sue you. Defamation is defined as *"the oral or written communication of a false statement about another that unjustly harms their reputation."*

Your ex can take legal action against you for defamation. Before you create an Instagram post defaming your ex, think twice.

Interfering with their work

"Revenge is a dish best served cold." Sounds familiar? The reality is that you got hurt, and you are blaming your ex-partner for it. Maybe instant retaliation isn't your thing, and you want to settle the score someday. Watch what you plan to do.

If you want to seek revenge by interfering with someone's work or livelihood, you might find yourself on the hook for serious legal consequences. Never call your ex's boss and tell them defamatory things about your ex to get him or her fired. This is something for which legal action **can** be taken against you. After all, you are interfering with someone's livelihood.

Breaking the lease

Anger can compel you to do things that you might regret later, like writing a letter to your landlord, explaining how you and your ex-partner have been breaking the terms of use of the apartment. Do you think you are just breaking the lease? You were a tenant too. That means any resulting legal action could affect you as well!

Should you change locks?

Whether the romantic relationship ended amicably or in a chaotic situation, your personal safety should be a priority. You may have asked your ex to hand over their keys to your place. Have you stopped to think if they made copies of the key after they realized the relationship was doomed? If so, then changing the locks is a good decision.

However, not every situation is so straightforward. For instance, your partner might be on the lease. If you change the locks on them, they can pursue legal action against you. The law will hold you responsible for the costly locksmith services.

Stealing from your ex

This is a no-brainer. Don't steal their expensive watch, car, computer, or anything else. Otherwise, he or she can take legal action against you. There is no reason to justify stealing their possessions.

Releasing raunchy images

Many people assume that the moment a relationship ends, their private photos (AKA "nudes") with their ex perish. Unfortunately, those nudes you gifted your ex in the past are likely to be safe, forgotten, and floating around his or her iCloud.

If you have such photographs of your ex, just delete them. Never release such content to public forums or social networks. Depending on the country in which you live, your ex might take legal action against you. Also, he or she can post your nudes as retaliation. Neither of these consequences are good for anyone!

Hacking their email

Reading someone's emails or other forms of confidential communication without their consent is illegal, so hacking someone's email, social media accounts, and electronic devices is illegal. He or she can pursue legal action against you.

As I said earlier, actions have consequences. You can regret some of your actions and make the necessary changes in the future. However, some actions are associated with very damaging consequences. Don't take chances. Just avoid any choice that could result in regrettable or long-lasting consequences.

Do's after a breakup

Here are the things that you can, and should, do after a breakup.

Establish boundaries

When a person has been in your life for quite some time, it might be very challenging to cut them out completely. Perhaps you and your previous partner have mutual friends, share various activities, work together, or have a class together. Knowing how to establish healthy boundaries with your ex-partner is essential.

Many people have dealt with this issue successfully, and these boundaries vary from person to person. What worked for your best friend might not be the right option for you. Therefore, you should follow your gut when choosing the best path for your mental, emotional, and physical healing after a breakup. Here are a few tips to help you establish healthy boundaries after a breakup:

Understand the importance of boundaries: If you still don't see the importance of setting boundaries between you and your ex, then you and I have many things in common. And one of those things is that we are both wrong! Establishing boundaries is essential for every relationship, particularly one that's experiencing turbulence or has just ended.

Clear, healthy boundaries will give you all the time you need to grieve, recollect yourself, and figure out what you want. They are there to help you and your ex navigate the aftermath of a breakup without feeling like you are drowning. Healthy boundaries touch on sensitive issues such as whether you will be talking, how often you will contact each other, whether you will continue to follow each other on social media, and more.

There is a long list of situations that are likely to change after a breakup. Though it might sound awkward, establishing boundaries and setting expectations of how you and your ex will handle various issues is important. It will make your life much easier in the long run.

Limit contact for some time: Even when you are absolutely sure you and your ex intend to maintain a healthy friendship, some time apart will not hurt. Take a break from texting, calling, or even hanging out together. You need some time to focus on yourself and heal. Taking some time apart will also help you avoid falling into a harmful pattern of providing emotional support to your ex and prolong the breakup.

Maintaining contact with your ex means you are still dedicating your energy towards a relationship that you no longer need. You may not be consciously aware of it, but that's the reality. Every time you work to make contact, you're simply siphoning off the energy you need to heal and pursue new life experiences.

Get to know and respect each other's needs: Do you want to maintain a friendship with your ex-partner? Have you checked with them whether they want to do so? Maybe your ex doesn't want it, and you keep on bothering them. That's not cool. Get to know what he or she wants and respect their choices. Don't send your mutual friend to talk to your ex about something you want. It is okay to miss your ex, but failure to respect their preferences will make things hard between the two of you.

In case your ex makes contact before you are ready to resume communication, do not feel obliged to go along with it. This can be very challenging, particularly if they express feelings similar to yours or sound vulnerable over the phone. Remember why you decided to take some time away and why your previous partner must respect that. You are supposed to focus on yourself and make strides towards healing. Wait until your preferred no-contact period passes before you establish contact.

Emotional and physical distance: A little breathing room might be the opportunity for you to turn things around and get over a breakup. Emotional and physical distance is healthy. Being alone doesn't mean you have to be lonely. Instead, it is an opportunity to nurse your heart and feelings. It makes you more independent, stronger, and presents a unique chance for personal growth.

During the months or years you were with your partner, your hobbies and interests may have been pushed aside. Taking some time for yourself allows you to pursue the interests and hobbies that you had previously tossed aside. Whether it's hitting a yoga class twice a week, catching up with a couple of pages in your favorite book club novel, or learning how to play the violin, you now have enough time to pursue what you love.

Also, you will have space and time for your relatives and friends. Perhaps you used to spend much of your free time with your significant other. With him or her glued to your side, you had less time to reconnect with your loved ones and friends. The relationship has ended. It's a bad thing. At the same time, you can push your ex away and let in people who appreciate you just the way you are.

If you still want to stay in contact with your ex after a breakup, keep a keen eye on old patterns and behaviors. For example, he or she pays you a visit and you realize they are leaning on your shoulder when watching a movie, just like old times. At first, you might think there is nothing wrong with this simple gesture. However, they can cause confusion and further emotional pain. The moment you decide to be friends, act like friends. Some of the habits you may want to avoid include cuddling, treating each other to expensive dinners, spending a night in the same bedroom, offering consistent financial and emotional support, and all other forms of close contact that reignite the idea of getting back to each other.

Talk about how you will handle encounters: There will be situations where you cannot avoid your ex-partner. If you attend college classes together, work together, or share many friends, there is a good chance you will meet frequently. It's recommended to discuss how you will handle these unexpected encounters. Focus on keeping things as simple and as polite as possible.

Take Care of Yourself

Now that you have the right boundaries in place, it's time to take care of yourself. Here is how:

Prioritize Self-Care

Create a daily self-care timetable. Some of the fun activities you can add to your schedule include:

- Activities that help you work out your feelings, like talking to someone close or a therapist, updating your journal, music, or art.

- Activities that nurture your health. For example, cooking your favorite healthy meal, meditating on positive things, and exercising.

- Activities that give you joy, such as your favorite hobby, experiencing something new, and going out with friends.

Sleeping is also good, but you shouldn't sleep too much as it can make you feel unwell and tired, and possibly interfere with other duties.

Occasionally it's good to have a glass of wine, some good food, and watch your favorite Netflix shows in the process of recovering. But be careful, so you don't become addicted to such habits and as a consequence, have a hard time leaving them. It would be best to preserve these things for occasions like when you are with friends or one day every two weeks to enjoy yourself.

Do the Things you Enjoy Most

Relationships are time consuming, and that means after a breakup, you have plenty of free time. Involving yourself in doing positive things during this time is essential.

You probably love reading, so you bought many books you hadn't managed to read because you only had a little time to spare when you were in a relationship. Or maybe you desired to learn how to cook or interior design. It's time to do that. When you engage yourself in doing things you enjoy, you easily overcome post-breakup grief.

You can also book a vacation with your friends to create new memories. The anticipation of going on your most awaited vacation will help you stave off bad emotions. Just don't invite your ex.

Express Your Feelings but Don't Wallow in Them

Emotions such as loneliness, confusion, grief, sadness, bitterness, anger, etc., are common when a cherished relationship dies. Acknowledging you are experiencing such feelings is helpful. Denying them will do more harm than good. Get a pen and paper and note those feelings. Afterward, talk to somebody close to you. Reading, listening to music, and watching movies of people who went through the same situation can also give you comfort.

Contemplating loss and grief doesn't help so avoid dwelling on these negative emotions. You may find it difficult to get your ex off your mind, and when that happens, it's good to reset your mind by involving yourself in a deep task like cleaning, listening to music, going to your friend's house, or going for a walk.

Avoid love songs, romantic or sad movies for some time. Rather, try lighthearted books without love stories, upbeat music, or comedy shows. Such will help you remain positive.

If you still feel low, try the following;

- Opening the curtains to let in some sunshine.

- Light a candle with a citrus or fresh scent.

- Take a shower with the products you love or let the shower water drop on you as you sing your favorite songs freely.

- Sit in the sun.

Write a short story about your breakup, even if it's one sentence. For example, *"I'm taking time off relationships until I reconnect with myself and my own needs."* You can also write, *"Things are not clear right now because it takes time to break up."* Stick those notes

112

somewhere you can view them with ease, for instance, on your fridge door and meditate on them whenever you think about your ex.

Reach Out for Support

It hurts to break up. Help from family and friends can help minimize feelings of loneliness. However, this isn't enough. Make an appointment with a therapist. Your therapist can help you do the following;

- Draw up a plan.

- Handle abuse or manipulation effects.

- Tackle persistent negative feelings.

- Point out unhealthy coping techniques and help you replace them with positive ones.

In case you think a breakup is not a good enough reason to see a therapist, I am afraid you are wrong. It is one of the significant areas therapists specialize in because they know the aftermath of a breakup can take a toll on your life.

If you have been experiencing the following, you must reach out for support:

- Think of calling your ex or keep calling them.

- Have suicidal thoughts or thinking of doing something to hurt yourself or others.

- Depression.

It takes time to heal from a breakup. However, patience is essential, and as time moves, it will become easier. For the time being, be gentle with yourself and seek help if needed.

Do a Digital Detox

You may need to block or unfriend your ex on social media. With such platforms, you may not avoid passive-aggressive bullying, unhealthy friction, or even cyber-stalking. In case you don't want to block or unfriend your ex, remember you can always *"re-friend"* them after you have healed. You can avoid social media at all costs, or if you still want to use social media, unfollow your ex's accounts, delete their photos and messages. If possible, also block their contact in your phone, as it will help you to stop expecting a call from them.

Be kind to yourself and ask questions like, *"Is this action beneficial to me right now?"* when you feel like checking their Instagram. The answer is **no**, and deep down you are aware of that. Instead, engage in activities that require your presence like sending an email to a family member or close friend. It will be challenging at first, but it *is* doable.

Redesign Your Physical Space

Redesigning your physical space will help you reset your mind. If you have been staying in the same house, plan to move out, if you can. If not, you can rearrange your living room, keep the photo of you two out of your sight, change your bedsheets, etc. This decreases the possibility of relapse.

Pay Attention to Your Thoughts

Once the raw pain has subsided, it is a good time to examine the relationship and reflect. This is the shakeup you may have needed to change the focus of your life. Several researchers say that breakups offer you a higher chance of listening to your inner self to see what you need to learn and how you can be more aware.

You may also feel you want to share your story with your friends. However, before you act on that, ask yourself, "How will it benefit me if I share?" or "What happens if they gossip about it (because they will)?" Fake friends will take sides and will jump at the chance to spread some gossip. So when you are tempted to talk to someone, choose someone you trust.

You may also think of letting your social media friends and followers know you broke up. You shouldn't. People who should know your relationship ended are most likely already aware, so avoid posting. This is most likely when your ex wronged you or cheated on you. However, instead of going public about it, it would help if you would share the information with only people you trust. You also don't want to stain your name, so don't spread rumors just to make yourself feel better.

Read a Good Book

You may struggle to move on after a breakup, but reading a good book can offer you great comfort. There are many books you can select from. The best choice for you will depend on your taste. When the breakup is raw, you may have few options of books you'd love to read, but as you heal, the scope will widen. Good books help you escape the situation. The insights you get from reading them enable you to process the situation while deeply engrossed in something different.

Steer clear of different forms of romantic distractions

It is tempting to just dive right into another set of arms after a breakup. However, this is like placing a band-aid on a fresh bullet wound. It is more like exposing a bullet wound to public restroom germs! Though most people still think that having sex with just anyone can help you get over a breakup, that's not the case. Instead of taking care of yourself, you are just opening the door to more issues.

Indeed, starting a new relationship before healing is a distraction destined to complicate your life more. It will be very difficult to deal with the consequences of these temporary or unplanned relationships. Even when you reactivate your tinder account, don't engage anyone. Just wait until you have healed to start dating.

Don'ts After a Breakup

The challenges of getting over a breakup will ease with time. Until then, avoid the common traps that could set you back:

Don't Have Breakup Sex

It's possible to desire to have sex with your ex after a breakup, but that's a terrible idea. It will build an emotional bond, and that will make it hard to get over them. Sex after a breakup reignites the good and bad memories. That's something you don't want.

Don't Stalk Your Ex on Social Media

You will want to check what they have been posting or whose photos they have been uploading on their accounts, mainly if you saw them with a new person in town. Perhaps you want to know if they feel bad about the breakup, or you want to see if they posted something directly attacking you. Resist the temptation. The urge to stalk them may be too high, but you can replace it with jogging or calling a friend, and the more you overcome that urge, the easier it becomes to get them off your mind.

Don't Rush into a Rebound Relationship

Trying to get over your previous relationship by getting into a new one is not a good idea. Perhaps you feel an emptiness that needs to be filled. But that space can't be filled by another person. You have to take time to heal; otherwise, you will just be on the road to another breakup.

Also, when you have not yet healed, you may appear too dependent or needy, and this can put off even a willing suitor. You may also find it challenging to trust your new partner, so it is good you avoid getting into a new relationship too soon.

Avoid a Breakup Haircut

Breakups are painful. You can go from having a good time on a vacation talking about your future together, and now you have an ex, and you are their ex. For some, this comes with a desire to change their appearance. You may have been desiring to do so, and now you have the chance to, or maybe it's revenge. If grief or pain motivates you to cut your hair, you have to evaluate whether that will make your choice valueless or add emotional baggage to your decision.

Maybe you think it will make you feel good because it's a change to a new style, but it can come with regrets. Most of the decisions you make when the breakup is raw aren't thought through well, and that's the reason you need to stop and heal first.

The desire to act against a breakup doesn't last forever, and when you have healed, you may wonder why you cut your hair. Especially if you are doing it because of your ex, then it is not the right choice.

Don't Obsess Over What Went Wrong

Thoughts of what went wrong in your seeming unshakable relationship are common after a breakup. Excessive, persistent images and thoughts are called obsession. These thoughts can make your healing process slower, in addition to causing anxiety and pain. If you have been experiencing the following, then you are obsessed with your ex.

- Neglecting family and friends.

- You can't sleep, eat, or focus.

- You defend yourself and say unnecessary things.

- You keep meditating about how charming your ex is and put aside all negative characteristics.

- You believe he or she is meant to be yours regardless of what happens.

- You have seemingly unending and uncontrollable crazed thoughts.

- All you talk about is your ex-partner.

- You are overthinking instead of focusing on the essential aspects of your life.

Obsession is associated with self-defending, controlling, and jealous actions. Feelings of anger, envy, betrayal, regret, guilt, and shame promote the preoccupied emotional condition. If that's what you are going through, you need to take action for your healing to be quick. It's a difficult task, but it's vital.

Don't compare yourself with other people

Everyone experiences a unique set of ups and downs in the wake of an emotional split. If you feel that you are facing more challenges than your best friend or taking longer to get over your ex, don't worry. It's completely normal. One pitfall you should avoid is comparing yourself to other people. Your friends, relatives, and colleagues have unique qualities and respond to issues differently. Comparing yourself to them leads you to believe that the aspects that differ must be negative.

The moment you realize something different, that's the beginning of a bigger problem. You will be demoralized and start perceiving yourself and the ability to make decisions negatively. With time, you will start feeling low and depressed. It's easy to develop the habit of comparing yourself to other people. Unfortunately, it's hard to break it. The last thing you want is an extra problem when dealing with a breakup.

The death of a meaningful relationship is one of the most hurtful events that can happen to you. However, when it happens, there are many things you can do (and other things you need to avoid) to speed up your healing. If only you can be disciplined in doing what's necessary and avoiding all the don'ts, you will have an easier time. There is a lot to enjoy in life that you can't afford to stay stuck in a broken relationship.

Chapter Seven: Rethink your Definition of Closure

"Closure" is a psychological term that describes one's strong desire for an answer to an aversion toward ambiguity. It is the motivation to find clarity and answers to ambiguous situations. The need for closure is enhanced by perceived benefits such as a stronger basis for action and being able to predict what might happen in your world. The imagined cost of lacking closure also enhances the motivation to find closure. Missing deadlines is an example of such costs.

The need for closure exerts its impact via two distinct tendencies, urgency and permanence tendency. The urgency tendency refers to the inclination to get closure within the shortest time possible. On the other hand, permanence tendency revolves around maintaining closure for a long time. When these tendencies merge, they create the inclination to seize and freeze on the earliest judgmental cues. This reduces the level of information processing and introduces a bias in thinking.

In the case of a breakup, closure means getting a clear understanding as to why the relationship didn't work. This process varies depending on the unique circumstances of a breakup and other factors. It is a unique experience.

Understanding closure

Imagine your lover unexpectedly changes their social media relationship status to *"Single"* and stops communicating with you. That sounds cruel, right? It's beyond any reasonable doubt that your partner has robbed you of the right to know why they left. In such a situation, it's possible to have a strong desire to know what happened (seek closure) and move on.

The need for closure also applies to other situations beyond romantic relationships. The loss of a job, death of a loved one, and other events with painful endings. Generally, letting go of someone or something that was once important is challenging. This is the reason most people seek closure.

Does closure help? Do you expect other people to help you find closure?

When you seek closure, you are simply looking for answers to the primary cause of the breakup to resolve the unbearable pain associated with that awful event. In doing so, you create a mental puzzle of everything that has happened while you were still in the relationship, during the breakup, and after the event. The details of each of the phases of your relationship become a huge piece of the puzzle that you feel compelled to solve. The closure will be achieved when you successfully analyze and solve the puzzle in your mind. That means the closure is equivalent to the specific answers you seek.

Many people seek closure because the reasons for the termination of the relationship are significant to them. The end holds some value and meaning to them. If you realize that your partner ended the relationship to begin a new one, you will find closure straight away. You don't need further explanation to understand the abrupt end to the relationship. However, if your partner just disappeared off your radar without explanation, it might take you longer to find closure.

Ultimately, getting answers regarding the painful ending can help you maintain your identity and learn a few things about yourself. This is one of the reasons some people often feel like they are better off choosing a partner with age. Also, elderly individuals take a somewhat more relaxed view about stressful events like death compared to young people. This is because elderly people had lost loved ones before and mastered the art of finding closure.

Every situation is different

The need for closure occurs on a scale. Some people are more likely to seek it, while other people avoid closure to the best of their ability. They probably don't want to amplify the pain associated with rejection, guilt, and criticism. Remember, vagueness comes with its benefits too. The moment you know the exact cause of the breakup, you will be subject to self-criticism and ridicule from other people.

The concept of closure is unique for everyone. What appears to be a satisfactory answer to your friends' issues may not be sufficient for your situation. After all, the reason your relationship ended isn't the same reason your best friend lost their job. That means one person's need for closure is a function of personality characteristics, values, and circumstances. Clearly, these parameters vary, and so does the need for closure.

Different personalities approach closure differently. For instance, people who prefer predictability and order (and have a rigid way of thinking) face difficulties if they don't find closure. On the other hand, people who are creative, more open-minded, and comfortable with ambiguity can cope better even when they don't find closure.

Also, people who find closure consistently have unique values that can easily incorporate the answers they find. These facts and opinions help validate their world. For example, a religious ideology explains many questions in one's life as *"God's will"* and no further explanation is needed for them.

The differences in people's need for closure plays a significant role in the potentially damaging impact of getting closure. These effects include questioning your judgment, abilities, and skills.

Why should you seek closure?

You may have heard that *"the only person who can give you closure is yourself."* It is a statement that's said defeatedly after one's ex has refused to explain what caused the emotional end of the relationship. Unsurprisingly, the mantra often comes as advice from family members, friends, and colleagues. These are the people who try to be sympathetic to you, particularly when going through a hard time.

That *"hard time"* might mean a one-sided breakup where the partner quitting the relationship acts indecently or rudely. In an attempt to shirk guilt and responsibility, they choose to explain to the other partner the reason for the breakup. This causes the rejected person psychological distress and pain. The notion that you can give yourself closure is prevalent because it gives an illusion of control. And the premise is essentially accurate – you are responsible for your own life.

Unless you know how to give yourself closure, this advice might do more harm than good. Just think about it. You suffered a loss, and you don't know why it happened. This can deplete your self-esteem. The advice to get your own closure may infuse the notion that you are now responsible for getting over a decision that you don't understand in the first place. The chances are that you will find it challenging to reconcile your emotions and navigate the difficulties associated with a breakup.

But why does having the reason for an emotional split matter so much?

Historically, humans understand the world through stories. You created your past, present, and future. You can navigate your unique world through cognitive structuring. Nearly all healthy relationships have a sense of where they have been, their current position, and where they're heading. In the same way, you should have a good sense of who you are and how you feel about each element of your story. When a breakup occurs, it interrupts your story, especially if you didn't expect it.

By understanding why the union ended, the partner who initiated the breakup will have already sorted out their story. Unfortunately, the other person is likely to be thrusted from a safe psychological territory into an abyss of psychological distress. A similar analogy can be created when you discover that your partner is transgressing the sanctity of a romantic relationship.

Getting closure after a breakup makes it easy to restructure your perception of your past, present, and future through understanding what happened and reconfiguring your story. If you don't get closure, attempts to understand the cause of the split will flood the conception of your past, present, and even the future.

You will be wondering, what did I do? Why would someone I trusted so much do this to me? Can I trust myself to make the right choices when past choices have caused me pain? Unless you get the answers regarding the breakup, your view of reality through past-present-future analysis will become warped. The chances are that you will lose the sense of what you know about yourself and the level of trust you had in yourself. Remember, this is mediated by one's social comparison, personality, mood, and attachment styles. Failure to get closure can worsen it.

As much as you want closure, don't pursue it to fill a selfish void. Don't focus on making your ex feel rejected and hurt. No matter how much emotional pain you are going through, insulting your ex and telling them how unfair or wrong they were won't fix anything. These are unfruitful attempts to fix your pride. You are just trying not to feel like a loser.

These attacks will sting your ex, but they will forget within a short time. They will spend very little time thinking about you. On the other hand, you will waste so much energy and time yelling and gain nothing positive. Find other ways to destress. For instance, you can join a yoga class.

Getting Closure after a Breakup

The best way to get closure after a breakup is to believe there is no chance of you two reviving the relationship. That is a commitment that is not easy to muster if you still believe there are chances of a reunion.

Even though you don't know what the future holds, holding anger will waste the time you should be healing. It is a good idea to embrace *"single-dom,"* because even though a breakup is hard to believe, it's not the end. Here are ways to find closure.

Accept you are not meant to be together

Today, people believe there is someone meant for them, which makes it hard to reset your mind that your ex wasn't meant for you. However, be honest with yourself and ask these questions: *"If this is the right person for me, then why was our relationship unhealthy and bad?"* The short answer is they, in fact, might **not** be right for you.

Of course, you have to feel you are meant for each other when you are beginning a relationship because otherwise, the relationship would not have kicked on. But remember, human beings change. Even if you were once meant for each other, changes could cause the person to no longer be the right choice.

How you frame the condition will determine whether finding another partner will be easy. There are many who are willing to hook up with you and with whom you can have a great relationship. The process isn't like searching for a needle in a haystack, but instead selecting the best cloth in a clothing store. You need to take time figuring out the best option if you want something outstanding.

Delete the contact of your ex

Cutting the cord will require you to delete the contact of your ex. It may feel bad because it's putting a finality to the connection between you and them. However, that finality is proper because you want to move on. It helps you turn your back on the broken relationship, and when the next suitor comes, you will have healed and will be ready to start a new relationship.

Block, unfriend and unfollow your ex on social media

There is a certain magic in social media that makes people feel together even when they live on different continents. Some people even stalk people they broke up with many years ago, which is dangerous. They are addicted to it and can't help but find out what their ex is doing, which hinders complete disconnection.

It will be helpful to unfriend, block, and unfollow them so you won't see what they post, as this could make you want to follow what they are doing with their lives.

After healing, date other people

Note that you should only get into another relationship once you have healed, so you can avoid rebound relationships. Move slow in this so you can make the right choice. Hanging out with friends, going on a vacation, etc., are ways you can create fresh memories and meet people you can comfortably date.

Your feelings matter a lot in this. If you are not yet emotionally stable enough to get into another relationship, you need to give it time. Some people struggle with trust issues after a breakup, and if that is the case, you may need to wait until you feel you are ready to trust again. However, note that if you take too long to date again, you may find it more difficult to do so.

If you still feel there is an emptiness that needs to be filled, you aren't ready. However, when you are happy without a partner, and are excited and aware of your emotions, you can go ahead and start dating.

Speak what you feel

This can be in written form or verbally to someone you trust. If you choose to put it down on paper, don't send it to anyone. Writing down what you feel is an excellent way of getting closure. You can burn or bury the letter later as a sign of ending the connection. If you choose to talk to someone, find a confidant whom you are not afraid of telling whatever you feel. Keeping stuff to yourself can make you keep ruminating on the negative, even after many years of separation.

Don't blame yourself or your ex

It could be your actions, or it could be your ex's actions that caused you to break up. However, playing the blame game is never a good option, because it does not solve anything. When you are wrapped up in the blame game, you cannot get closure. Let go and reset your mind to think about how to refocus your life.

Forgive

Forgive yourself and your ex; otherwise, you will still be drawn to think of the mistakes you or your ex made that cost you your relationship. Forgiveness also gives you peace. Resentment and blame are signs of not being able to forgive. Therefore, if you are experiencing them, you have to work on forgiveness. Some people cannot stand their own faces after a breakup because of blame. You don't need to get to that point.

It's hard to forgive, especially when you are convinced it was your ex who was wrong, but it's necessary to do it. Forgiveness doesn't imply what occurred is okay; instead, it's the willingness to let go. In the next chapter, you will learn how to forgive and find the chance to be happy once again.

Chapter Eight: Finally, Forgive and Move on

No one gets into a romantic relationship expecting a breakup. You let someone into your life because you have seen something in them that you really want to be part of. There is the attraction, both physical and mental, that draws you closer to that person. The bad news or good news (depending on the partner you ask), the relationship didn't last. For various reasons, the relationship ended.

There is a common relationship fantasy that doesn't involve getting physical. Instead, it's verbal. Its climax is not an orgasm. I'm talking about the ever-elusive concept of getting closure. In such a fantasy, maybe you are mustering up every perfect comeback at just the right moment, or berating your ex-partner for ghosting you. Or maybe you are visualizing how your ex would come back apologizing for how he or she hurt you and telling you that you were right in every argument.

This is a fantasy. And the reality is more frustrating than you think.

Do you remember what I said about getting closure? You might get it or you might never get it. How will you get it if you already know that your ex will not come back and apologize? What would happen if you never get closure? Does that mean you have to live with the pain of a breakup forever? It's time to face reality.

Instead of holding onto a severed relationship, you can recognize that it's time to let go, forgive, and move on.

Not everything must change

Everyone has sky-high expectations about love. Similarly, modern culture reinforces the notion that we are all owed (and shall receive) a fully satisfying sense of closure in the wake of an ended relationship. Culturally, there is a lot of conditioning, music, and television shows that emphasize the importance of having that pivotal conversation to resolve everything. You cannot count on that conversation and allow yourself to be held back.

When there are unresolved issues between you and your ex, it becomes a crutch for you not to feel vulnerable. You have created a story about a romantic relationship, and it appears you are still stuck there. This could be the reason you have so much anger that's holding you back from healing and getting over the breakup.

Well, change is an inevitable part of your life. Some changes are positive, while others are negative. Some are within your control, and others are out of your control. Many people are unhappy just because they cannot accept circumstances that are beyond their control. Eventually, they get frustrated and disappointed.

You need to focus your energy and time on the parts of your life that you can change and accept what you cannot change. After all, not everything needs to change. Whether you get closure or not, you can still find happiness within yourself. Realize that nothing lasts forever. This is the key to finding peace and happiness.

Swap up unhealthy habits with a healthy lifestyle

Yes, that's possible!

Everyone experiences happiness differently. For you, happiness may mean being at peace with who you are, securing a network of people who cherish you, and the freedom to pursue your passions. No matter the version of happiness you desire, living a more satisfied and happy life is within you. All you need is to swap bad habits with healthy ones. Here is how:

Smile

Swap anger with smiles. Generally, people smile when they are happy. This habit is a two-way street. Accumulating scientific evidence suggests that smiling causes the human brain to release dopamine, a chemical that makes humans happier.

This doesn't mean that you are supposed to plaster a fake smile onto your face at all times. You will look like a burglar is holding a gun on your head, and you are trying to show that you are very happy. It won't work. Instead, have a genuine smile. The next time you feel bored or low, crack a joke with your friends, smile, and see what happens. Or stand in front of a mirror, admire yourself, remind yourself how good you are, and **SMILE!**

Outdoor activities are the real fun

Regular exercise can help minimize feelings of anxiety and reduce stress and other symptoms of depression. Also, it can boost your happiness and self-esteem. Some of the activities you may want to consider include yoga, tai chi, daily walks, or 5-minutes stretching sessions every morning. You can either work out alone or with your friends.

Get enough sleep

No matter how your work and household chores steer you toward less sleep, you know that sufficient sleep is important to your physical, emotional, and mental health. You need seven to eight hours of sleep each night. If you ever find yourself feeling like you are in a fog or fighting the urge to nap after lunch, your body is telling you that you are not getting enough sleep.

Here are a few tips to help you get better sleep each night:

- Write down the number of hours you should sleep each day. After a week, evaluate your progress and how you feel.

- Specify the time you will be going to bed and waking up each day, even on weekends.

- Reserve 45 minutes or more as quiet time before you sleep. Take a bath or do something relaxing.

- Avoid drinking alcohol or heavy eating before you go to bed.

- Keep your bedroom cool, quiet, and a little dark.

- Invest in a high-quality mattress and bedding.

- If you want to take a nap during the day, limit it to 20 minutes.

If you cannot sleep consistently, or suspect that you have a sleep disorder, consult with your doctor. The point is, don't focus on the bad feeling or indulge in alcohol or other bad habits. No matter how angry you might be, swap those bad things with habits that can improve your overall well-being.

Try all things – find a hobby

For most people, carving out energy and time to engage in hobbies seems like something they don't have time for. Family, work, school, and other obligations can be time consuming, leaving less room for doing other things that you enjoy.

Hobbies can take you out of your everyday experience and offer you an opportunity to do something you are passionate about. It can be a good mental escape, it can create time to socialize with other people, or hone a skill. Hobbies are a unique way to disconnect from your schedule and do something that cheers you up.

Here are some of the benefits of hobbies and how they can contribute to your journey of overcoming a breakup:

Physical hobbies, such as swimming, martial arts, hiking, and camping, have many psychological benefits. They can increase your brain function and heart rate. Also, they can help boost your energy level, build muscle, lose weight, and balance your blood pressure.

Spending some time doing things that you love is a good way to improve your emotional and mental well-being. These activities reduce stress by taking your attention away from pressing issues and help you relax. For example, if you feel too overwhelmed by the pain of a breakup, activities like swimming, hanging out with your friends, or hiking can help you relax. Other helpful hobbies include coloring, gardening, photography, cooking, listening to music, and more.

Other hobbies involve social and interpersonal activities. They are a great way to connect with your friends, meet new people, and bond with people who appreciate you. Social activities add another layer of support to your daily schedule and reduce stress. Discussing philosophy, group dancing, playing games, and watching movies are some of the activities you can do as a group.

Some hobbies could inspire you to tap into your creativity. These include knitting, soap making, writing fiction, cake decorating, interior décor, and more. These activities can be helpful if you lack a creative outlet at your workplace. Remember, this creativity can extend to other aspects of your life.

Volunteering, meditating, journaling, and completing puzzles are hobbies that offer you the chance to improve your confidence and self-esteem. They can also improve your quality of life. Some of these hobbies might align with some of your long-term goals. For example, meditation can improve your emotional and mental health while volunteering presents an opportunity to learn a thing or two about leadership.

Getting over a breakup is a long, complicated journey. In addition to all other healing options and tips I have shared, your hobbies play a key role in minimizing the impact of a severed relationship. They present a chance of true happiness and self-development.

Time is your friend

The choice to forgive should arise from your desire to be at peace with yourself and other people around you. It is a multi-step process that happens over time. There is no specific period within which you should forgive your ex.

Forgive yourself

Stop jumping to conclusions that you were the cause of the split. Even if at some point you did something that led to the downfall of your relationship, it's now over. There is no point in blaming yourself for mistakes that you did or didn't make. It is unhealthy and unproductive to do so.

You have probably been sad for months, begged your ex to tell you what happened, and tried to reason with your friends to understand why the union didn't work. Finally, I am telling you what you don't want to hear – you cannot fix everything, and your previous relationship wasn't an exception. **Sometimes, there is no fix.**

Rather than beating yourself up, focus on yourself, and forgive. Just forgive yourself for all the things you wish you had not done, the harsh words, and most importantly, forgive yourself, because no one is perfect. Everyone makes mistakes.

That may sound preachy and oversimplified, but it's the truth. Your main goal in life shouldn't be to never make mistakes. Instead, you should learn from the mistakes you do make, make the necessary adjustments, and live a peaceful life. Take some time alone, think about the broken relationship, and forgive yourself. As long as your heart beats, you still have a chance to live a better life.

Forgive your ex too

This is the most challenging part of getting over a breakup. He or she hurt your feelings, wounded your self-esteem, and battered your pride. Are you supposed to forgive such a person? I understand why you would find it hard to forgive them.

From the start of this book up to this point, you have realized that the key to getting over a breakup is focusing on yourself. I am now asking you to forgive your ex. Not because they deserve it, but because you deserve a happy, peaceful life. By forgiving them, you acknowledge the fact that no one is perfect. Let's be honest. When you look back and analyze your life, you will realize that you have also made mistakes. I have made mistakes too, and so has everyone else. That's part of being a human.

The main reason to forgive your ex-partner is that holding on to pain and anger is unhealthy. It will make you bitter. No one wants to be around a bitter person. So forgive them, because you want to have a happy day at work, hang out with your friends, and get a good night's sleep. Forgive because you deserve physical and mental health, because you want to achieve your academic goals, and because soon you will meet a suitor who will love you dearly.

At some point in life, everyone has experienced unmet expectations. Hanging on to those painful experiences keeps people from enjoying their precious lives and soaring up the social ladder. Don't let the pain and anger cloud your judgment and miss the opportunity of being a happy person.

<u>Just let go.</u>

Conclusion

You fought a good fight, and finally, you have decided to forgive and move on. The time has come to let go of the pain and anger. You will learn not to think twice about being single or feel lonely just because you are not dating. Isn't that an awesome feeling?

Hold on to that feeling. Have faith in yourself that you will be happy. The possibility of emerging from a breakup happy, healthy, and strong depends on how well you implement the steps you have learned in this book. Have you accepted what happened? Have you detoxified digitally, rebuilt your self-esteem, and avoided pitfalls that could drag you back to self-blame? And most importantly, have you forgiven yourself and your ex?

Look ahead, several years down the line, and visualize the kind of person you will be. You will thank yourself for reading this book and learning how to get over a breakup.

I wish you all the best in your future journey but more than this, I wish you happiness.

Sources

1. Macdonald G, Leary MR (2005) Why does social exclusion hurt? The relationship between social and physical pain. Psychol Bull 131:202–223. CrossRef

2. Scientific American Mind. (2013, May 1). How Does the Brain React to a Romantic Breakup? https://www.scientificamerican.com/article/how-does-the-brain-react-to-a-romantic-breakup/

3. KRAVITZ, J. K. (2018, October 25). How Does A Breakup Affect Your Brain? Studies Show It's Fascinating. Elite Daily. https://www.elitedaily.com/p/how-does-a-breakup-affect-your-brain-studies-show-its-fascinating-12974577

4. University of Hertfordshire. (2014, March 7). Self-acceptance could be the key to a happier life, yet it's the happy habit many people practice the least. *ScienceDaily*. Retrieved July 22, 2020 from www.sciencedaily.com/releases/2014/03/140307111016.htm

5. Taylor Ph.D, S. T. (2013, April 8). The Power of Acceptance. Psychology Today. https://www.psychologytoday.com/us/blog/out-the-darkness/201304/the-power-acceptance

6. REYNOLDS, S. R. (2014, March 27). 8 Of The Realities You Must Accept When Mending Your Heart After A Breakup. Elite Daily. https://www.elitedaily.com/dating/sex/8-of-the-realities-you-must-accept-when-mending-your-heart-after-a-breakup

7. Bell, L. B. (2017, August 14). Escape Tech: What Is A Digital Detox, How And Why To Do One And Where To Do It. Forbes. https://www.forbes.com/sites/leebelltech/2017/08/14/escape-tech-what-is-a-digital-detox-how-and-why-to-do-one-and-where-to-do-it/#1a5103f2912c

8. DownTime87. (n.d.). Digital Detox Benefits – What To Do After

A Breakup, Featuring Amy Chan. https://downtime87.com/digital-detox-benefits-what-to-do-after-a-breakup-featuring-amy-chan/#:~:text=The%20aftermath%20of%20a%20breakup,move%20forward%20with%20your%20life.

9. KEMP, J. K. (n.d.). Rushing Into a Relationship After a Long-Term Relationship. Classroom. https://classroom.synonym.com/hallmarks-signs-rebound-relationship-16807.html

10.   Juth, V., Smyth, J. M., & Santuzzi, A. M. (2008). How do you feel? Self-esteem predicts affect, stress, social interaction, and symptom severity during daily life in patients with chronic illness. Journal of health psychology, 13(7), 884–894. https://doi.org/10.1177/1359105308095062

11. Grande Ph.D., D. G. (2018, January 26). Building Self-Esteem and Improving Relationships. Psychology Today. https://www.psychologytoday.com/us/blog/in-it-together/201801/building-self-esteem-and-improving-relationships

12. Alpert, J. A. (2014, March 21). The Dos and Don'ts of Getting Past a Breakup. Huffpost. https://www.huffpost.com/entry/the-dos-and-donts-of-getting-past-a-breakup_b_5000378

13. Caraballo, J. E. C. (2018, July 9). *Is it Possible (or Necessary) to Get Relationship Closure?* Talk Space. https://www.talkspace.com/blog/relationship-closure-possible-necessary/

14. RITTER, B. R. (2017, July 17). The Science Of Closure And If You Really Need It. Elite Daily. https://www.elitedaily.com/dating/science-closure-need-it/2002103

15. Sekendur, B. S. (n.d.). Healing, Forgiving, and Loving After a Painful Break Up. Tiny Buddha. https://tinybuddha.com/blog/healing-forgiving-and-loving-after-a-near-death-break-up/

141